The UN Convent... and Children's Rights in the UK

The UN Convention and Children's Rights in the UK

by
Peter Newell

For the National Children's Bureau in collaboration with the
Calouste Gulbenkian Foundation

ISBN 0 902 817 77 9

Published by the National Children's Bureau
8 Wakley Street
London EC1V 7QE
Telephone 071 278 9441

Typeset, printed and bound by Saxon Printing Ltd, Derby.

The National Children's Bureau was established as a registered charity in 1963. Our purpose is to identify and promote the interests of all children and young people and to improve their status in a diverse and multiracial society.

We work closely with professionals and policy makers to improve the lives of all children but especially children under five, those affected by family instability and children with special needs or disabilities.

We collect and disseminate information about children and promote good practice in children's services through research, policy and practice development, publications, seminars, training and an extensive library and information service.

Contents

Part II
Implementing the Convention Worldwide

Preface

The National Children's Bureau as a child-centred organisation is frequently critical of the way children are regarded in our society. All too often their needs and interests are submerged by the concerns of adults, whether professionals or parents.

For many people in the United Kingdom the adoption by the United Nations in November 1989 of the Convention on the Rights of the Child was seen as being of particular relevance to other countries, especially those in the Third World or Eastern Europe, rather than our own. That was not a view that we shared.

Instead, we welcomed the Convention as an opportunity for all of us to do more to promote the rights of children. We saw the need to examine the articles of the Convention to identify what they meant for UK legislation and practice and we decided that Peter Newell, with his breadth of knowledge about children's rights, was the ideal person to carry out this study on behalf of the National Children's Bureau.

The report that Peter has produced shows not only the gaps but also the real progress that has been made in recent years culminating in the Children Act 1989. Nonetheless, as the report shows, there is still much more to be done. We hope that the publication of this report will help all those working for or with children to improve their policies and practice.

The British government has indicated that it will ratify the Convention on the Rights of the Child. We are glad of that commitment but wish that the process of ratification could have been speedier so that Britain could have been a leading force in implementing the Convention. We hope that the government will use this study to assist it in framing its legislative programme and policy development so that children's rights can be centre stage in the future.

Barbara Kahan
Chair
National Children's Bureau

The author

Peter Newell is Coordinator of 'EPOCH' – End Physical Punishment of Children'. A writer and advocate for children's rights, he previously worked at the Children's Legal Centre and Advisory Centre for Education.

His publications include *Children are People Too – The Case Against Physical Punishment* (Bedford Square Press, 1989); *A Last Resort? Corporal Punishment in Schools* (Penguin, 1972) and – with Martin Rosenbaum – *Taking Children Seriously: A Proposal for a Children's Rights Commissioner* (Gulbenkian Foundation, 1991).

He lives in London and has three children, Matthew, Joe and Finn aged six, four and one.

Acknowledgements

Responsibility for the text of this book is entirely my own. But it could not have been written without the help of many individuals and organisations in the children's field, among them the following to whom I would like to express warm thanks:

Susan Alexander; Fran Bennett; Professor Jonathan Bradshaw; Christopher Cloke; Ros Finlay; Bob Franklin; Professor Michael Freeman; Zarrina Kurtz; Ruth Lavery; Penelope Leach; Kathleen Marshall; Audrey Moser; John Quinliven; Martin Rosenbaum; Philippa Russell; Sue Shutter; Mark Vaughan; Barbara Ward.

Staff of the National Children's Bureau.

Advisory Centre for Education; British Agencies for Adoption and Fostering; British Red Cross; Child Accident Prevention Trust; Child Care Northern Ireland; Children in Development; Children's Legal Centre; Coalition on Young People and Social Security; Commission for Racial Equality; Family Care, Edinburgh; International Association for the Care and Resettlement of Offenders; National Association for the Welfare of Children in Hospital; National Association of Citizens Advice Bureaux; National Association of Young People in Care; National Children's Home; National Society for the Prevention of Cruelty to Children; National Youth Bureau; Refugee Council; Re-unite; Save the Children Fund; Scottish Child Law Centre; Voluntary Council for Under Fives; Wales Advocacy Unit, the Children's Society; We Welcome Small Children Campaign; Youthaid.

Introduction

Children's rights have come of age! The United Nations Convention on the Rights of the Child, adopted by the UN General Assembly on 20 November 1989, now provides detailed minimum standards against which to test treatment of the world's two billion children and young people.

Many millions of the world's children are preoccupied solely with the fight for survival in conditions of grinding poverty and ill health. Every day 40,000 children die from malnutrition and disease. Millions of others live on, only to find themselves involved in wars or threatened by environmental hazards which adults – not children – have created. Individual children in every society are exploited, abused, neglected, or simply ignored by adults.

Children lack any effective voice in political systems; even, generally, in the services and institutions designed exclusively 'for' them. They face unique discrimination on grounds of their age and status, and many face the double jeopardy of additional discrimination on grounds such as disability, race, culture, gender, class and poverty.

The Convention provides a new focus to concentrate the world's attention on its children. UNICEF's Executive Director, James P Grant sees it as embodying a fundamental principle:

'That the lives and the normal development of children should have first call on society's concerns and capacities and that children should be able to depend upon that commitment in good times and in bad, in normal times and in times of emergency, in times of peace and in times of war, in times of prosperity and in times of recession.'

We all bear responsibility for the world's children, and the UN Convention should be of concern to us all. It is there to be used to give all children a better deal. Each country's obligations under the Convention are not just to 'their' children. The Convention emphasises the need for international cooperation to give reality to the rights it guarantees throughout the world; the obligation of resource-rich nations, including the UK, to help developing countries meet obligations to 'their' children. The UK's recent record in working for the world's children is not impressive (see page 16).

But our outrage at how the world treats children, at how our own or other governments may treat children, should not blind us to the details of our own daily personal relationships with the children we live or work with: do they bear examination in relation to the principles embodied in the Convention?

While the UN Convention is not enforceable in the way that, for example, the European Convention on Human Rights is, it does provide internationally-accepted minimum standards which can be used, if necessary, to exhort, encourage or embarrass governments, authorities, institutions and individuals which fail to meet them.

It can be used in the UK, together with other relevant international and European instruments which potentially protect children, including the European Convention on Human Rights, to test and if necessary to help challenge laws, policies and practices. Little of the Convention is totally new: most of its provisions are included in other conventions and covenants. But it draws together these scattered principles and adds others specific to children: perhaps the most important are the obligation to seek children's views and take them seriously (Article 12), and to make the best interests of children a primary consideration in all actions concerning them (Article 3).

The Convention does place a prime responsibility on governments: to work for 'their own' children, and to work together with other governments for the world's children. The modest exercise which has produced this book must be pursued by government comprehensively and continuously. Ways must be found to ensure that the interests of children and young people, and the views of children and young people, are built into policy-making at every level. Some countries have already created independent governmental offices to promote children's rights and interests – a Children's Rights Commissioner or ombudsperson: such ideas are gaining support in the UK.

Over recent years, there has been substantial progress in some aspects of children's rights in the UK. In England and Wales, the Children Act 1989 represents the largest reform of children's law for decades; if implemented effectively and with adequate resources it will do much for children. There are current reviews of children's law in Scotland and Northern Ireland. But progress has been far from systematic across all services, and there is concern in particular at family poverty, and the equity of standards for children in the health and education services.

There is one major obstacle to implementation of many aspects of the Convention in the UK – a lack of information. There is only patchy monitoring of the state of the UK's children. The lack of consistently collected information makes it hard to judge precisely how changes in social and economic policies are affecting children and young people.

Reforms for children all too often come about as the result of some scandal, some exposed abuse, rather than through a comprehensive look at existing policies and practices. This can lead to haphazard and inconsistent changes: protecting children in one category of institution from particular abuses, for example, while leaving identical children in other institutions still at risk.

Another major obstacle to effective change is the lack of coordination of policy at central government level where many different departments (often appearing not to talk to each other) are responsible for different services, or different bits of the same service, for children. The same lack of coordination is reflected at local level.

Children and young people have no voice in our political system. They cannot vote until they are 18 (although they can fight and die for their country). They cannot be elected as MPs or local councillors until they are 21. The Convention is one instrument that can help us all – governments, authorities, organisations and individuals – to improve the status of children, and to ensure that they are treated seriously and accorded rights as people.

When will our political parties give children the central place they deserve in policy development? Could the next general election be the first to be fought on parties' varying commitments to children?

Purpose of the book

This book aims to help those working with or for children or living with children in the UK to get the maximum value out of the

Convention. In relation to each article it raises issues in relevant law, policy and practice which appear to breach the letter or the spirit of the Convention; it also gives positive examples of progress for children where appropriate. It is in no sense a legal commentary, and it does not pretend to be comprehensive. In particular, it may have failed to cover comprehensively the distinct legal framework and policies applying in Scotland and Northern Ireland.

The book seeks to raise enough practical examples to bring the Convention alive, to show how all of us in work with or for children can use the Convention as an instrument for policy development. For example, it can be used practically as a basis for drafting more detailed charters of rights for children in particular situations, or institutions, incorporating and developing its principles; it is a new instrument for auditing law, policy and practice. But the Convention must be seen as a set of minimum standards – indeed in some areas, our legislation and practice already far exceed these standards.

As this book goes to press (June 1991), the UK Government has not yet ratified the Convention. But it is committed to doing so soon. Most recently, the Foreign and Commonwealth Office indicated that, following wide consultations among government departments, it had agreed the areas of policy over which it would be necessary to make reservations when ratifying (see page 181).

Ratification will be an important step, signifying a new level of commitment to children's rights. We should all seek to ensure that it marks the beginning of a new era for the UK's children, and for our concern for the world's children.

Background to the Convention

The origins of the new UN Convention on the Rights of the Child can be found in the basic principles for children's welfare and protection set out in the 'Declaration of Geneva' promulgated in 1924 by the then Save the Children Fund International Union. This first attempt to codify basic children's rights was endorsed by the League of Nations. In 1948 it was revised and amplified, and formed the basis of the ten-point Declaration on the Rights of the Child which was adopted by the General Assembly of the UN on 20 November 1959.

'Declarations' are statements of general principles to be accepted by governments, but carrying no specific obligations. 'Conventions' are binding, requiring an active decision by states to ratify them. Until the Convention on the Rights of the Child was adopted in 1989, no binding international instrument existed bringing together states' obligations to children. But during the gradual development of universally accepted principles of children's rights, there was continuous development of international humanitarian and human rights law, much of it applying equally to children as people, and some of it containing specific provisions about children (for example, the International Covenants on Civil and Political Rights and on Economic, Social and Cultural Rights, and the Geneva Conventions). Over 80 binding and non-binding international instruments are concerned in one way or another with the rights of children. For children in the UK and other European countries, the European Convention on Human Rights provides particularly important safeguards (see Appendix 4, page 188). Its provisions apply without age limit, and individuals can make applications alleging breaches of the Convention, which are dealt with through the European Commission of Human Rights and the European Court of Human Rights in Strasbourg.

On the eve of International Year of the Child (1979) Poland launched a proposal for a Convention on the Rights of the Child. A Working Group was set up by the UN Commission on Human Rights during the year. The Group normally met for one week each year in January, immediately before the annual sessions of the Commission. In 1988, in order to finalise the whole draft text, the meeting was exceptionally extended to two weeks.

The Working Group was composed of representatives of the 43 member states of the Commission, which includes the UK. Delegates from other member states of the UN were able to participate as observers and play a full part in debate. Intergovernmental agencies like UNICEF, the International Labour Organisation and the United Nations High Commissioner on Refugees, as well as non-governmental organisations (NGOs) which had consultative status with the UN Economic and Social Council, could also be represented and participate in discussion of the draft. Working Group meetings were open to the public.

An ad-hoc group on the drafting of the Convention was formed, with Defence for Children International acting as secretariat. This group played a very active role in the drafting process.

Once the Working Group had agreed a full draft text, this was subjected to a detailed technical review, to ensure that it contained no internal contradictions and did not contradict other instruments, and that its language was correct. Then the Commission on Human Rights approved it and forwarded it to the UN Economic and Social Council. From the Council it went to the General Assembly of the UN in New York, where it was adopted unanimously on 20 November 1989, just 30 years after the adoption of the Declaration on the Rights of the Child. Javier Perez de Cuellar, UN Secretary-General, told the General Assembly:

> 'With the Convention on the Rights of the Child, the United Nations has given the global community an international instrument of high quality protecting the dignity, equality and basic human rights of the world's children.'

The Convention was officially opened for signature on 26 January 1990. Signing the Convention is a first step, an indication that a state intends to consider the Convention properly, as a prelude to possible ratification (the UK signed the Convention soon after adoption). Signing does not commit a state to ratifying the Convention. A month after ratification by the first 20 states, on 2 September 1990, the Convention came into force.

To date (June 1991), the Convention has been ratified by 90 states. A further 49 states have signed it but not yet ratified it. Only 31 states have neither signed nor ratified it. The UK Government is committed to ratifying the Convention. A Foreign Office Minister indicated in March that following Whitehall scrutiny of the Convention, consultations with UK Dependent Territories and Islands were taking place with the aim of moving 'as quickly as possible' towards ratification. The Government has indicated the areas of policy over which the UK is likely to make reservations on ratifying (see page 181).

Part I
Implications of the articles of the Convention for the UK

Definition of a child

Article 1

'For the purpose of the present Convention a child means every human being below the age of 18 years unless, under the law applicable to the child, majority is attained earlier.'

For the purposes of the Convention, childhood ends and majority is achieved at 18 at the latest. Throughout the UK the age of majority is 18. The wording of the Convention leaves open the starting point of childhood – is it birth, conception or somewhere in between? The deliberate intention was to avoid entangling the Convention in debates concerning abortion, embryo research and other highly charged issues which might well have threatened its adoption in many countries. But the Preamble to the Convention (see full text in Appendix 1, page 158) repeats the provision in the UN Declaration of the Rights of the Child, adopted on 20 November 1959, that 'the child, by reason of his physical and mental immaturity, needs special safeguards and care, including appropriate legal protection, before as well as after birth'.

Article 41 (see page 151) makes it clear that the Convention does not interfere with any domestic legislation (or applicable international law) which is 'more conducive to the realization of the rights of the child'. Thus the Convention's definition of childhood in Article 1 does not affect, for example, realisation of many 'adult' rights for young people throughout the UK at 16 or before, rather than at 18. For example, the Convention does not affect, for those under 16, the positive implications for self-determination of the 'Gillick' decision: that once children are judged to have 'sufficient understanding' they have the right to make decisions for themselves on important matters (unless there is a statutory age limit).[1] Similarly, the Convention does not affect the distinctive rights in Scotland of minor children – girls from 12 and boys from 14.[2]

Age of majority

Adoption of the Convention makes it an appropriate time to compare international policies on basic children's rights. In considering Article 1 it is worth noting that while in some countries 21 remains the age of majority, recently adopted constitutions in both Nicaragua and Brazil allow young people to vote from the age of 16. Extending voting to 16 and 17-year-olds in the UK would add about 1,800,000 young people to the electoral roll.

The article also provides a context for considering whether our laws currently delay adulthood, and the rights that go with it, beyond 18. There are a number of examples in the UK. Sexual activity between men remains an offence until the age of 21; in contrast, the age of consent for heterosexual activity for girls is 16, and the law does not specifically legislate on consensual sexual activity between girls or women. Our variable ages of consent clearly discriminate against homosexual young men aged under 21.

Young people cannot become local councillors or MPs until the age of 21 (although in certain Scottish local authorities young people over the age of 16 can vote in elections for local community councils, established under the Local Government (Scotland) Act 1973, and also stand for election); nor can they hold a licence to drive a large passenger vehicle or heavy goods vehicle (although they can hold a pilot's licence at the age of 17) or apply for a licence to sell alcohol.[3]

Rights without discrimination

Article 2

'1. The States Parties to the present Convention shall respect and ensure the rights set forth in the Convention to each child within their jurisdiction without discrimination of any kind, irrespective of the child's or his or her parent's or legal guardian's race, colour, sex, language, religion, political or other opinion, national, ethnic or social origin, property, disability, birth or other status.

2. States Parties shall take all appropriate measures to ensure that the child is protected against all forms of discrimination or punishment on the basis of the status, activities, expressed opinions, or beliefs of the child's parents, legal guardians, or family members.'

Article 2(1)

Article 2(1) insists that the rights included in the Convention are available without discrimination 'of any kind' against the child or his or her parents or legal guardians. It should therefore be read in conjunction with every other article in the Convention. (And in this book the implications of Article 2(1) will be addressed under every other appropriate article.) The article highlights the 'double jeopardy' suffered by many children and young people, discriminated against not only on account of their age and status, but also on other grounds such as disability, sex, race and colour.

The article also insists on an active rather than passive role for the State: to 'respect and ensure' the rights without discrimination. Systematic monitoring of services for children and young people, placement decisions, the use of sanctions and so on are required to determine whether groups are suffering discrimination. For example, there is inadequate collection of ethnic data, and monitoring and evaluation of it, to ensure that no racial group of children or young people is treated less fairly than others.

The list of grounds for discrimination mentioned in the article differs significantly from that in a similar article (Article 14) of the European Convention on Human Rights (see page 191) by including disability. For the UK, this emphasises the lack of any domestic legislation barring discrimination on grounds of disability: each of the rights in the Convention needs to be looked at from the perspective of children and young people in the UK with disabilities and learning difficulties.

In relation to discrimination on grounds of gender, there is a clear example in Scottish law: the age at which young people achieve the status of 'minority', with a consequential increase in capacity to make decisions for themselves, is 12 for girls but 14 for boys. The Scottish Law Commission produced a report in 1987 including a draft Bill which would eliminate the discrimination, but also remove certain existing rights of self-determination from Scottish young people up to the age of 16. The Bill was introduced as a private members' Bill (the Age of Legal Capacity (Scotland) Bill) in April 1991.

Non-marital children

The reference to discrimination on grounds of 'birth and other status' raises the issue of non-marital children (previously labelled 'illegitimate'). In England and Wales, the Family Law Reform Act 1987 removed most grounds for discrimination against these children, and in Scotland the Law Reform (Parent and Child) (Scotland) Act 1986 had similar effects. But it is still the case that British citizenship cannot be transmitted to a child by the father if the parents were not married to each other at the time of birth (see also Article 7, page 23). There is also discrimination over rights to succeed to titles and honours. The Scottish Law Commission has proposed changes which, if implemented, would remove the remaining discrimination against non-marital children in Scottish law. In Northern Ireland, no similar reforms have yet been implemented.

Wardship

While wardship can act as a form of protection for children's rights in England and Wales (see below), the 'status' of ward of court also carries with it a degree of discrimination for the child. Because all major decisions about a ward's life must be referred to the High Court, the child loses certain rights. Wards have no right to be parties or present at hearings, and once parties, no right to instruct a lawyer. And the High Court would appear to have greater powers than parents: it has been suggested, for instance, that the High Court can make decisions on medical treatment even for children over 16. (The Family Law Reform Act 1969 gives other young people the right to consent or withhold consent to medical treatment from the age of 16.) On occasions the High Court has prohibited wards from having contact with specified other people.[4] The implementation of the Children Act will mean that the number of wards will dramatically diminish. Their court rights under new court rules are still undecided (June 1991).

Article 2(2)

The State's action in detaining children because of the immigration or nationality status of their parents would appear to breach this article. In punishing (for example, imprisoning) parents the State must ensure that children do not themselves suffer punishment or discrimination. There are other ways in which activities of parents could cause discrimination or punishment to their children: for example, activities which caused their internment during hostilities. Racial harassment of parents can deeply affect children. Children of travellers are at risk of discrimination and harassment. In all such cases the State has a duty to take 'all appropriate measures' to protect children: this implies active concern and intervention.

The Child Support Bill, as presented to Parliament in February 1991, allows for a parent's benefit (income support, family credit, and so on) to be reduced in the event of failure 'without good cause' to provide certain information about the 'absent' parent (clauses 5 and 22). If implemented unchanged, this punishment of the parent (which will only be applicable to parents receiving certain benefits) will discriminate against the children involved, and could indeed cause them real hardship.

At an institutional level, the spirit of the article would be breached, for example, by a decision in a school to penalise children on the basis of their parents' refusal to attend a meeting.

Wardship remains available as a method of intervening to protect children against extreme beliefs or activities of parents which could lead to punishment or discrimination (for example, parents' refusal on religious grounds to consent to certain 'necessary' forms of medical treatment for a child unable to give consent for himself or herself). For England and Wales, S. 8 of the Children Act 1989 gives courts the power to make specific orders about aspects of

children's upbringing, which could also be used for such
interventions.

Best interests of the child

Article 3

'1. In all actions concerning children, whether undertaken by public or private social welfare institutions, courts of law, administrative authorities or legislative bodies, the best interests of the child shall be a primary consideration.

2. States Parties undertake to ensure the child such protection and care as is necessary for his or her well-being, taking into account the rights and duties of his or her parents, legal guardians, or other individuals legally responsible for him or her, and, to this end, shall take all appropriate legislative and administrative measures.

3. States Parties shall ensure that the institutions, services and facilities responsible for the care or protection of children shall conform with the standards established by competent authorities, particularly in the areas of safety, health, in the number and suitability of their staff as well as competent supervision.'

Article 3(1)

The insistence in the first paragraph of this article that the child's 'best interests' should be a primary consideration in all actions can only be fully satisfied when it is written into the legislation controlling such actions. The article lists actions undertaken by 'public or private social welfare institutions, courts of law, administrative authorities or legislative bodies.'

In some cases our domestic law already exceeds this test: for England and Wales, for example, Section 1 of the Children Act 1989 states:

'When a court determines any question with respect to – (a) the upbringing of a child; or (b) the administration of a child's property or the application of any income arising from it, the child's welfare shall be the court's paramount consideration.'

Similarly, the Law Reform (Parent and Child) (Scotland) Act 1986 states:

'In any proceedings relating to parental rights the Court shall regard the welfare of the child involved as a paramount consideration and shall not make any order relating to parental rights unless it is satisfied that to do so will be in the best interests of the child.'

In Northern Ireland, Section 48 of the Children and Young Persons Act (NI) 1968 provides that every court dealing with children or young people brought before it shall have regard to their welfare, and Article 17 of the Domestic Proceedings (NI) Order 1980 provides that the court must regard the child's welfare as the first and paramount consideration in deciding whether or how to exercise its powers concerning the child's custody or upbringing.

But by no means all 'courts of law' affecting children are bound by a 'best interests' principle. Criminal courts dealing with 17-year-old offenders are under no obligation to consider best interests in England and Wales, but the current (June 1991) Criminal Justice Bill will extend the principle (in S. 44(1) of the Children and Young Persons Act 1933) up to the age of 18. In Scotland children's hearings (available normally up to the age of 16) are bound by a 'best interests' principle.

Tribunals hearing immigration and nationality appeals (which frequently 'concern children') are not bound by any best interests principle. Nor are social security tribunals, which may hear appeals from young people aged 16 and 17, or the tribunals in the education system which make decisions on appeals concerning school choice, special educational needs and school exclusions. (As yet untested is whether the welfare principle binds judicial reviews examining an administrative decision affecting a child's upbringing.)

Outside the courts there are also huge gaps in fulfilling the implications of this article. The most glaring are in the education system: there is no duty to observe the best interests of the child in education legislation.

While it may safeguard children from particular hazards, legislation on health and safety and on environmental issues contains no basic principle on the best interests of children who may be affected. Nor does the planning system or legislation concerning planning inquiries and appeals mention children's interests. In housing legislation, there is no best interests principle to use to challenge, for example, the placement of children in 'bed and breakfast' accommodation.

'Administrative authorities' includes local authority services. The Children Act 1989 insists (S. 17) that local social services authorities in England and Wales shall 'safeguard and promote the welfare of children within their area who are in need', and also (under S. 22(3)) of children they are looking after. (The Act has, however, removed the previous obligation to give 'first consideration' to the welfare of the child.) But social services authorities may act inconsistently with this and other basic duties towards children they are looking after 'for the purpose of protecting members of the public from serious injury' (S. 22(6),(7) and (8)). Section 27 enables, for the first time, social services to require assistance to be provided by, for example, health, education and housing authorities, unless it prejudices the efficient discharge of the latter's duties. But these Children Act duties apply to children 'in need' – not to all children in the authority's area (and authorities may interpret 'in need' very narrowly). The Scottish Child Care Law Review Report suggests that local authorities in Scotland should be required to assist any child where it appears that such assistance will promote the child's welfare.[5]

The Children Act has gone a long way towards ensuring that public and private social welfare institutions (but not, generally, education institutions) in England and Wales act in the best interests of the child. Institutions provided and administered by social services departments (such as community homes) are covered by the welfare duty referred to above. The Act also places duties on voluntary homes (S. 61(1)(a)), registered (private) children's homes (S. 64(1)(a)) and boarding independent schools (S. 87(1)) to 'safeguard and promote the child's welfare'. But curiously, non-maintained special schools – an anomalous group of schools which are neither state schools or independent – are not covered by this legislation, and nor, of course, are maintained schools. Regulations applying to residential care homes (mostly for elderly people but also including children with disabilities and learning difficulties) contain a similar welfare principle.

The legislative framework for the National Health Service and its institutions – hospitals, mental hospitals, adolescent units, and so on – lacks any principle concerning the best interests of children receiving treatment. The basic duties in health legislation are concerned with securing improvements in physical and mental health, and the prevention, diagnosis and treatment of illness. And although the legislation applying to private health institutions (nursing homes and mental nursing homes) has recently been revised, no welfare principle has been inserted for children. The ethical principles governing the medical professions do imply a first duty to the patient's welfare, but such principles do not cover the administration of health institutions.

The Human Fertilisation and Embryology Act 1990 (see Article 7, page 26), when first presented to Parliament, made no mention of the interests or rights of children born as a result of 'artificial' methods of conception. But a modest amendment was added so that Section 13(5) does make it a condition for providing 'treatment services' to a woman that:

> 'account has been taken of the welfare of any child who may be born as a result of the treatment (including the need of that child for a father) and of any other child who may be affected by the birth.'

Within the penal system, too, there is no 'best interests' principle, either in primary legislation or in rules applying to penal institutions for young people (the young offender institutions).

In Scotland, no such principle applies to services or institutions for children and young people, except in relation to local authority services for children in care (S. 20 of the Social Work (Scotland) Act 1968).

Article 3(2)

This, together with Article 9, covers the state's overriding obligation to ensure the provision of necessary protection and care for children and young people, in particular when parents or others responsible fail to do so. The obligation to provide 'adequate care' suggests the need for standards for local authority care, and powers for central government to intervene when necessary. Section 84 of the Children Act gives the Secretary of State in England and Wales the power to intervene when satisfied that an authority has failed to comply with a duty under the Act. And the National Health Service and Community Care Act 1990 broadens these powers to cover all social services functions, and provides the Secretary of State for Scotland with powers to issue directions to local authorities (S. 50 and 51).

Children's own rights to seek care and protection remain limited. At present (June 1991) in England and Wales children can approach social services and ask to be received into care. The local authority can receive them into 'voluntary' care if satisfied that their parents are unable to care for them and that it would be in their best interests, but parents can discharge their children from voluntary care. Children cannot apply to court for compulsory care proceedings (social services, police, NSPCC and education authorities currently (June 1991) can, as can parents of children beyond control). Under the Children Act, due to be implemented in October 1991, children get no new rights to refer themselves to care, except that 16-year-olds can place themselves in local authority accommodation (even against parents' wishes). The police and local education authorities will no longer be able to apply for care orders and parents will have no means of doing so. In Scotland, children can take refuge in a place of safety and thus initiate compulsory care proceedings subject to the discretion of Reporters to Children's Panels (and in Northern Ireland, too, children can take refuge in a place of safety).

Children who are estranged from their parents, and children on the run from their parents and from care and penal institutions would fall under the protection of this article, which suggests that more specific obligations to provide care and protection should be enacted; the state should take over when parents have failed to provide adequate care. Section 51 of the Children Act 1989 for England and Wales provides some supporting safeguards for providing refuges for children who may be 'at risk of harm': safe houses for children and young people who have run away from their home or from an institution. These can provide a positive period to negotiate with adult support if needed, some resolution to the problems. In particular, 16 and 17-year-olds no longer have a right to social security (see page 102); they may also have problems with renting accommodation.

Article 3(3)

This paragraph places obligations on the state to maintain standards through adequate inspection. It also implies the existence of standards, and presumably consistent standards, in institutions, services and facilities providing 'care or protection' for children. Here again, the Children Act and regulations and guidance being issued under it have made great strides towards providing consistent and detailed safeguards for children placed in many institutions outside their family home in England and Wales. But there are still substantial gaps and inconsistencies. Health and safety legislation, for example, only applies to employees, so that in schools it does not protect pupils, or in hospitals patients.

While the state does, through Her Majesty's Inspectorate of Schools (HMI), inspect independent schools, no standards applying to all independent schools are laid down in law. The Children Act (S. 87) places duties on social services to ensure that the welfare of children in independent boarding schools is adequately safeguarded and promoted, and there will be regulations to cover inspection by social services. The Act also ensures that independent schools which accommodate less than 50 pupils (and are not approved for use by children with statements of special educational needs) are subject to dual registration, as schools and as children's homes (S. 63(6). When the Act is fully implemented in 1991, these particular independent schools will, as registered homes, be subject to extremely detailed regulations which, for example, prohibit the use of physical punishment and other undesirable sanctions. Other independent schools, approved under the Education Act 1981 for use by children with statements of special educational needs, are covered by another, different and less rigorous, set of regulations.[6] (None of this detailed legislation applies to independent schools in Scotland or Northern Ireland, but current reviews are likely to lead to similar changes.)

In the health sector, too, there is no detailed legislative framework of inspection and standards to safeguard children in either the NHS or the private sector.

New safeguards for children in private and local authority foster care will also be implemented for England and Wales under the Children Act; to conform with this article, they must provide adequate and consistent standards and monitoring procedures.

In Scotland and Northern Ireland there are at present no detailed safeguards for children and young people living in the wide variety of institutions available (but current (1991) reviews may lead to them). In Northern Ireland, the independent inspection units which have been monitoring statutory, voluntary and private residential homes since 1 April 1991 will eventually take over responsibility for inspecting all children's homes. The remaining inconsistencies clearly breach this article, which should encourage the Government to look again at the whole spectrum of institutions in which children spend significant periods, and ensure that the safeguards applying to them are consistent and sufficient.

Implementing rights in the Convention

Article 4

'States Parties shall undertake all appropriate legislative, administrative, and other measures, for the implementation of the rights recognized in this Convention. In regard to economic, social and cultural rights, States Parties shall undertake such measures to the maximum extent of their available resources and, where needed, within the framework of international cooperation.'

This article ensures that states ratifying the Convention are obliged to take 'all appropriate legislative, administrative and other measures' to implement the rights for children in it (see also Article 42, page 154, which obliges states to make the Convention's principles and provisions well known to adults and children by 'appropriate and active means').

Article 4 and other parts of the Convention make clear that states are not expected to have implemented the Convention fully by the time they ratify; ratifying signifies an intention to fully implement (subject to any reservations individual states may enter (see page 181)), and an ongoing commitment to ensure that new legislation or policy does not breach the Convention. Clearly the Government should have a permanent procedure for ensuring that any proposed new legislation complies with the UN Convention, the European Convention on Human Rights and other relevant instruments.

International cooperation

The article also contains an acceptance of the wide variation in resources available to different states for implementing the Convention: with respect to economic, social and cultural rights they must undertake measures 'to the maximum extent of their available resources'. But it is important to note that this does not apply to the civil rights guaranteed in the Convention. The last sentence of the article gives states a duty to help others implement the Convention through international cooperation. Taken with the last paragraph of the Preamble (which recognises 'the importance of international cooperation for improving the living conditions of children in every country, in particular in the developing countries'), this gives resource-rich countries such as the UK a responsibility to respond to the needs of poorer countries. In many parts of the world, the basic rights of millions of children to an adequate standard of living, health care and education are denied. Forty thousand children worldwide die every day, most from causes that could be prevented cheaply and easily if the resources were made available.[7]

In terms of economic wealth the UK is certainly rich. But its direct contribution to international cooperation to improve the state of the world's children is disappointing in comparison with that of others. The most commonly used index of official development assistance is the percentage of gross national product (GNP) devoted to aid. In 1989 the UK figure was 0.31 per cent. The UN target figure is 0.70 per cent. In the UK the present Government (June 1991) has not set a timetable for reaching the UN target. The UK also compares badly with other OECD/Development Assistance Committee countries, ranking thirteenth out of 18.[8]

The article also suggests consideration of how much of UK overseas aid reaches children around the world and thus supports the implementation for them of the rights set out in the Convention. This is difficult to assess on currently available information. But the amount of aid given by the UK to UNICEF, which is specifically mandated to meet the needs of children worldwide, has fallen in recent years, from £15.4 million in 1987/88 to £9.3 million in 1989/90.

Debt is a major factor preventing poor countries from being able to meet the needs of their children. About 85 per cent of the world's 1,800 million children aged under 16 live in developing countries. The developing world's debt stands at approximately $1,300 billion. Julius Nyerere, former President of Tanzania, asked: 'Must we starve our children to pay our debts?' The UK should play its part, through international cooperation, in solving this problem.

Parents' rights and duties

Article 5

'States Parties shall respect the responsibilities, rights and duties of parents or, where applicable, the members of the extended family or community as provided for by the local custom, legal guardians or other persons legally responsible for the child, to provide, in a manner consistent with the evolving capacities of the child, appropriate direction and guidance in the exercise by the child of the rights recognized in the present Convention.'

This article suggests that parents' rights and duties to provide 'direction and guidance' for their children must be exercised 'in a manner consistent with the evolving capacities' of their children. This would seem to reflect the principle, established in the Gillick case[9], that once children are judged to have acquired 'sufficient understanding' they are empowered to make decisions about important things for themselves, unless specifically barred by statute. Under the article the state must respect parents' 'responsibilities, rights and duties' if properly exercised. The House of Lords decision in the Gillick case also made clear that any rights parents have over their children derive from their responsibility to promote their children's welfare, and are limited by that responsibility. The principles established in Gillick would take precedence over this article, in that they are 'more conducive to the realization of the rights of the child' (see Article 41, page 151).

In a recent Discussion Paper on parents' responsibilities and rights, the Scottish Law Commission suggests that in reforming Scottish law, there should be a general statutory statement of parental responsibilities because

'it would counteract any impression that a parent has rights but no responsibilities and ... it would enable the law to make clear that parental rights are not absolute or unqualified, but are conferred in order to enable parents to meet their responsibilities'.[10]

The Children Act 1989 recognises the rights of the child to a 'parental' relationship with non-parents: the courts in England and Wales will be able to award residence orders (care and control) and contact (access) rights to third parties. The article emphasises the need to respect varying family and parenting patterns.

The Criminal Justice Bill currently (June 1991) before Parliament proposes to allow courts in England and Wales to place new obligations on parents of children under 16 brought before them and convicted of criminal offences. This includes (clause 48), with the parents' consent, ordering them to enter into a 'recognisance' to 'take proper care of' and 'exercise proper control' over the young person. If parents refuse unreasonably, they may be fined up to £1,000. Many commentators regard these provisions as an unconstructive state intervention in parents' obligations towards their children; do they amount to the 'respect' by the State which this article demands?

The State's obligations to support parents in their parenting duties are covered by Article 18 (page 64).

The child's right to life and development

Article 6

'1. States Parties recognize that every child has the inherent right to life.

2. States Parties shall ensure to the maximum extent possible the survival and development of the child.'

There is no fundamental duty in line with this article in health legislation (Article 24 covers other health issues (see page 90)). Lack of clear standards and adequate monitoring of children's health services makes it difficult to judge how effectively the article is implemented in the UK. Such information as is available – for example, infant mortality-rates – suggests that there are wide and discriminatory variations in implementation by region, social class, and ethnic origin. The Department of Health is currently reviewing guidance on children's health services which may provide new standards.[11]

Over the last few years, groups of medical specialists responsible for various services to children have publicised their concerns. For example, attention has been drawn to the fact that in some parts of the UK, new-born babies' access to intensive care cots and appropriate specialist nursing staff has decreased. In many areas it falls well below the levels of provision recommended by the British Paediatric Association and British Association of Perinatal Paediatrics.[12] An article in the *British Medical Journal* in July 1990, for example, collected data from 17 perinatal units in the Trent region, and found that £600,000 was needed immediately to provide satisfactory levels of monitoring and supportive equipment for the units.[13] The Paediatric Sub-committee of the North West Regional Health Authority, commenting on the shortfall in numbers of intensive care cots available in the region in 1988, and the result of taking another five cots out of service at a Manchester hospital, stated: 'The paediatricians in the North West Region believe that this reduction in service will mean that more of these very sick infants will die or survive with handicap'.[14] A report from the Royal

College of Physicians on *Medical Care of the Newborn in England and Wales* in 1988 stated bluntly in its introduction: 'Without the necessary resources, many babies who could have been rescued will die and, as was the case 25 years ago, a high proportion of the survivors will have avoidable handicaps.' While the report acknowledges that the neonatal survival rate of babies of very low birthweight has very significantly increased, it indicates that when last surveyed (in 1984) there were only 473 fully staffed and equipped intensive care cots, against a recommended number of 729. 'Failure to implement previous reports has led to present services developing in a haphazard way with wide variations between different regions'. Those professionally involved 'remain concerned that the needs of ill newborn babies are still not adequately being met':

> 'Many critically ill babies born in district maternity units cannot be properly accommodated in neonatal intensive care referral centres because of lack of adequate resources in those centres. Some babies are accommodated after a delay, others have to be transferred long distances to referral centres in other regions, and some remain in their hospital of birth and are deprived of the urgent care they need'.[15]

The report emphasises that neonatal intensive care is not an experimental form of treatment, 'but a necessary life-saving procedure'. The introduction to the report asks: 'Finally ... is the question of whether we can better afford the economic cost of providing appropriate standards of care for ill newborn babies or the moral cost of failing to do so...'.

Other groups of consultants have questioned our ability to maximise the survival and development of very ill children. The United Kingdom Children's Cancer Study Group in their Report on cancer services for children, in 1987 warned: 'we are entering a phase when we may no longer be able to offer children the best available care and some will die who might otherwise survive'.[16] Consultants and others at one of the supra-regional centres for infant cardiac surgery told their regional health authority in 1988 that if the shortage of specialist intensive care nurses was not relieved, 'we foresee an extremely dangerous situation where increasing numbers of both adults and children will die on increasingly long waiting lists'.[17]

The European Commission of Human Rights has confirmed that Article 2(1) of the European Convention on Human Rights (which begins: 'Everyone's right to life shall be protected by law.' – see page 188) 'enjoins the state not only to refrain from taking life "...intentionally...", but, further, to take appropriate steps to safeguard life'.[18] The Commission was commenting on an application made by an association representing parents whose children had died or suffered lasting or severe damage as a result of vaccinations. The Commission rejected the case, finding that it could not be said that 'the state has not taken adequate and appropriate steps to protect life'. But it did look in some detail at the system of control and supervision over the vaccination and immunisation programme in the UK.

It is clear that if this article of the Convention is to be adhered to, we cannot allow existing services to deteriorate, and (reading the article in conjunction with the anti-discrimination Article 2 (see page 4) we must ensure that children's right to life and to maximum survival and development does not vary unnecessarily according to the region they live in or their parents' class, ethnic origin or circumstances. In 1987 rates of stillbirth and death at various stages in the first year of life in England and Wales increased progressively from occupational classes 1 to 5, from 6.9 per thousand live births to 11.8, with an overall rate of 8.0. There are also wide recorded differences in infant death rates according to the mother's country of origin: in 1987, the infant death rate among women born in Pakistan was 15.2 compared with 8.5 among Bangladeshi-born mothers, 7.0 among East African-born mothers and 8.9 among British-born mothers. Regional variations in the rate are also substantial: in 1987, there were 6.6 per thousand live births in the East Anglia and Mersey Regional Health Authority areas, 7.3 in Wales, and as many as 9.7 in North East Thames and 10.1 in Yorkshire.[19]

All these differences raise issues of discrimination when Articles 6 and 2 are read together. In October 1990 the Department of Health announced that there had been further improvements in the overall infant death rates for 1989, but that disparities between regions persisted. Regions have been asked by the Department to ensure they each have at least one pathologist specialising in paediatric pathology and to consider the need for further posts. They are also conducting surveys into trends in illness and mortality in infants.[20]

A report published by the National Children's Bureau in 1987, emphasised the link between social and material deprivation and children's health problems:

'Rates of perinatal and infant mortality, child abuse, cigarette smoking and drug addiction all go up in direct proportion to rates of unemployment, homelessness and poverty. Poor perinatal care and immunisation failure are also more common among the most socially disadvantaged groups. We would be failing in our duty if we did not point out that improvements in social conditions would make a greater impact on child health than is likely to occur as a result of any re-organisation of professional work'.[21]

The links between deprivation and health need to be considered in relation to Articles 26 and 27 on children's social security rights and standards of living (see pages 101 and 105).

Name and nationality

Article 7

'1. The child shall be registered immediately after birth and shall have the right from birth to a name, the right to acquire a nationality, and, as far as possible, the right to know and be cared for by his or her parents.
2. States Parties shall ensure the implementation of these rights in accordance with their national law and their obligations under the relevant international instruments in this field, in particular where the child would otherwise be stateless.'

UK children have a right to a name when registered; registration must occur within six weeks of birth. Current legislation on naming children is discussed under Article 8 (page 28).

Principle 3 of the UN Declaration of the Rights of the Child, adopted in 1959, and still in force, states: 'The child shall be entitled from his birth to a name and a nationality'. The current Convention only refers to the right to 'acquire' a nationality. Until implementation of the British Nationality Act 1981, on 1 January 1983, all children born in the UK were British citizens (except children of diplomats). That Act abandoned the principle of citizenship by birthplace. Since then, a child becomes a British citizen at birth only if the child has a British citizen parent or a 'settled' parent (that is, with the right to remain in the UK indefinitely): if married, either parent's status counts; if non-marital, only the mother's status counts (if the parents marry at any time after birth, the child will acquire British citizenship). The inability to acquire British citizenship through a British father is a clear form of discrimination against non-marital children born in the UK.

Stateless children

Since the Act came into force in 1983, each year several thousand children are born in the UK who do not acquire British citizenship. In many cases they will take the nationality of one or other parent's country, under the law of that country. But some children will get neither British citizenship nor the citizenship of parents, because countries have different laws on conferring citizenship on a child born abroad. Such children will be 'stateless'.

Children not born British in the UK have a right to register as British citizens if, after their birth in the UK, their parent becomes a British citizen or achieves 'settled' immigrant status; or if the child has lived in the UK for ten years and has not been absent for more than 90 days in any one of those years, he or she can register between the ages of 10 and 18. A non-citizen child adopted in the UK by a British citizen, or jointly by a couple one of whom is a British citizen, will become a British citizen (but a 'settled' adoptive parent does not make the child a British citizen, which discriminates against adopted children in relation to the acquisition of nationality). In addition, a child born stateless will become entitled to register as a British citizen between the ages of 10 and 22 if it is shown that he or she has always been stateless, has spent five years in the UK immediately before the application and has not been absent for more than 450 days out of the five years. The Home Secretary has further discretion under the Act to register any child who applies but is not otherwise qualified for registration under the Act. There is no obligation to give reasons for refusing an application for discretionary registration.[22] Whether this discretion amounts to a 'right' to acquire nationality for all children born here, as required by Article 7, seems doubtful.

A child who is adopted overseas by a British citizen has no right to acquire British citizenship or to come to Britain to join his or her parents, even where the overseas adoption orders are recognised under British legislation. This is discriminatory when compared with a child born of British citizen parents living abroad who themselves gained their citizenship in the UK: such a child does have a right to acquire British nationality.

The child's right to know his or her parents

The child's right to know his or her parents, qualified in this article by the words 'as far as possible', is a particular issue for adopted children, and also for those conceived by 'artificial' means (such as donor insemination or *in vitro* fertilisation). For children of married parents, there is an assumption in law that the husband is the father; where this is known not to be the case, the article suggests that children have a right to know 'as far as possible'. For non-marital children, a mother can enter the father's name on the birth certificate by agreement, but the father has no right to enter his name without agreement, unless there is proof of paternity and a court order. This discretion again conflicts with the child's right to know his or her father 'as far as possible'. (It appears likely that proposals in the Child Support Bill, currently (April 1991) before Parliament may lead to fathers' details being entered on birth certificates less often – see page 108).

Adopted children

Adopted children have no right to information on their biological parents until their eighteenth birthday (in Scotland, adoptees have had this right at the age of 17 since 1929), when they have access to any names and particulars of parents shown on the original birth certificate. (If the adoption was made after 12 November 1975, this information will only be made available after the young person has been counselled; in Northern Ireland this applies to those adopted after 1 October 1989.) But this article insists that 'children' – that is, those under 18 – have a right to know their parents. In Scotland, adults who were adopted have a right of access to their court file: such information would appear to be part of a child's identity which this article and Article 8 (see page 28) give him or her a right to 'preserve'.

In England and Wales, under the Children Act 1989, the Registrar General is required to set up an Adoption Contact Register, to enable adopted people to contact their birth parents and other relatives. But this will only be open to those aged 18 or over (the Government sought to introduce an amendment while the Children Bill was in Parliament to enable adoptees under 18 years of age to lodge information with the Register, but this was opposed by organisations seeking to protect adoptive parents' interests, and dropped). The Registrar General will provide, at the request of an adopted person who has registered with him, the name and address of a relative who has asked for details to be placed on the register.

In Scotland, a 'Birth Link Register' was established by the organisation Family Care in 1984: it provides a computerised register on which people involved in the adoption 'triangle' (for adoptions registered in Scotland) can register their own wish for contact, and record information about themselves. In a submission to the current 1991 Inter-Departmental Review of Adoption Law, Family Care says:

'In our work ... we see an increasing number of adult adoptees who have been driven by the need to know who they are and where they come from, as we all need a sense of our roots ... Many enquirers call at Family Care in a state of utter distress, having for the first time (sometimes at the age of 40 or 50 years) just found out they were adopted. We may not be able to stop this happening for past adoptions, but consideration ought to be given to safeguarding the children being placed now and in the future, from this devastating experience'.

Family Care recommends that:

'the rights of children should include the right of access to knowledge of their pre-birth and pre-adoption identity and the responsibilities and duties of parents should include those of ensuring that that right is fulfilled insofar as it is possible'.[23]

(Also relevant to this article and Article 8, the organisation states that many adoptees have indicated that they were upset to find that their adoptive parents changed the forename given to them by their birth parent – see page 28)

Adoption law for the whole of the UK is currently (1991) under review. This Inter-Departmental Review must include consideration of the age at which children should be entitled to 'know their parents', in the light of this article. The age could, for instance, reflect the Gillick principle – that children acquire a right to the information when judged to have 'sufficient understanding'. Current limits on disclosure would appear to be there for the benefit of parents – both biological and adoptive – and not necessarily those of children.

'Donor' children

For those born as a result of artificial techniques of fertilisation (in the UK in 1988 approximately 4,000 by all methods), before implementation of the Human Fertilisation and Embryology Act 1990 (likely to be implemented in 1991) there are no rights to information about genetic parentage. After implementation, there will be no rights to information until the age of 18 (except that those aged 16 or over and about to marry will be able to seek information as to whether they might be genetically related to their proposed spouse). At 18 there will be very limited rights, set out in regulations not yet issued (June 1991), to information collected by the Human

Fertilisation and Embryology Authority. This will include confirmation as to whether they were born following the use of donated gametes, and some non-identifying information about the donor's physical and personal characteristics. (Those who have been deceived about the method of their conception will, of course, have no reason to seek information from the Authority. The Royal College of Obstetricians and Gynaecologists has advised prospective donor insemination (DI) recipients: 'unless you reveal [DI conception] to your child, there is no reason for him or her ever to know that he or she was conceived by donor insemination'.[24]

In Sweden, legislation does give donor children a right of access to the identity of their genetic father when known. There are concerns that in the UK children's rights have not so far been given sufficient consideration in drafting this legislation. Arguments in favour of donor anonymity and secrecy clearly conflict with the child's right to know and have so far been regarded as paramount. Adopted children have the right of access at 18 to all the information recorded about their parentage. But donor children will not have access to all the information contained in records to be maintained under the Human Fertilisation and Embryology Act, and are thus discriminated against in relation to adopted and all other children. The Act does say that children's welfare must be considered before providing a woman with 'treatment services' – see page 11.

To fulfil the implications of this article, the only limitations on a child's right to know his or her parents should be practical ones: 'as far as possible' means the child should have a right to any information which it is possible to collect and which has been recorded. This is a very complex area of law, and one in which new issues may well arise, but the law should certainly be reviewed in relation to the right implied by Article 7.

NOTE: The Government has indicated that in ratifying the Convention it is likely to enter reservations about this article (and Articles 2, 9 and 10) in order to protect the working of UK nationality and immigration law (see Appendix 2, page 181).

Preservation of child's identity

Article 8

'1. States Parties undertake to respect the right of the child to preserve his or her identity, including nationality, name and family relations as recognized by law without unlawful interference.

2. Where a child is illegally deprived of some or all of the elements of his or her identity, States Parties shall provide appropriate assistance and protection, with a view to speedily re-establishing his or her identity'.

It appears that parents in the UK have the right to seek to change the nationality of a child without any obligation to consult the child or obtain the child's consent.

UK parents have a duty to register a child within 42 days of birth and to give the registrar a surname by which it is intended the child will be known. Forenames must also be given if they have been chosen. A parent can change or add names but only within 12 months of birth. Parents who adopt a child have the power (subject to the court's approval) to change the child's name, in which case the new names are entered in the adopted children's register held by the Registrar of Births. This effectively replaces the original birth certificate. A shortened form of birth certificate can be obtained which makes no reference to the child's biological parents or to the adoption. Again, while courts in adoption have an obligation to consider the ascertainable wishes of the child, the child has no right to retain his or her name (see also Article 7, page 26).

The section of the birth register recording details of the child's father can be completed only at the joint request of the mother and father, or on proof of paternity by a court order. Thus a child may be denied knowledge of his or her father's identity.

While the registered name cannot be changed after the age of one (except by adoption) a child or parent can use a different name. But there does not appear to be any legislation defending the child's right to have his or her registered name used if their parents wish to change it. If parents disagree about the name by which a child should be known following separation or divorce, and the matter has to be decided in court, under the Children Act 1989 there would be an obligation to take account of the child's wishes, but no obligation to follow them. In the absence of specific legislation on children's rights to change their name, it would appear that the Gillick principle should apply: that once judged to have sufficient understanding they should be able to make a statutory declaration changing their name (the alternative procedure of filing a deed poll with the High Court is only available from the age of 16).

The child's right to preserve family ties, protected by this article, appears to conflict with current adoption law (currently under review) and practice, in which the child on adoption usually loses normal rights of contact with biological parents, brothers, sisters and other birth relatives (and, to the age of 18, information about them, see page 25). While there is an obligation to ascertain the child's wishes concerning a proposed adoption, the child's consent is not required. (In Scotland there is a requirement for capable 'minor' children – girls from 12 and boys from 14 – to consent in addition to parents, thus there is discrimination on this issue within the UK (see also Article 2, page 4).)

While the Convention does, of course, allow for separation of children from parents where necessary in the interests of the child (see Article 9, page 32), the unnecessary separation of a child from, for instance, his or her brothers and sisters during placement in care would breach this article. The Children Act 1989 (S. 23(7)) gives local authorities a duty to place siblings who they are looking after together, so far as is 'reasonably practicable' and consistent with the children's welfare. In Scotland regulations applying to residential placement and foster-care placement have similar effect.

Access to files

The child's right to 'identity' has been found to include a right of access to files containing personal information. Rights of access by children and young people to records and reports written about them by the whole range of professionals and others involved in education, care and treatment should be revised in the light of this article (the linked issue of controlling others' access to such information is considered under Article 16, page 60).

There has been significant progress in the last few years (despite, in many cases, strong professional opposition) towards upholding children's own independent rights of access to their reports and records; in particular in relation to social services, and in the health service children have a right of access, with certain exceptions, to records in these services on request, if judged able to understand 'the nature of the request'. In education, in contrast to social services and health records, regulations on school records only provide young people with a right of access from the age of 16; below that age parents have a right of access. The general rights of access for subjects of data kept on computers given by the Data Protection Act 1984 were specifically limited to prevent children who were the subject of a statement of special educational needs under the Education Act 1981 having access to their statement if it was stored on computer (although their parents – not the 'subject' of the statement – do have rights under the Education Act 1981 to the statement and accompanying reports).

In a recent case before the European Court of Human Rights, brought by Graham Gaskin, a young man who had been in care from before his first birthday and was denied access to social services files, the Court stated that people in his position:

> 'have a vital interest, protected by the [European Human Rights] Convention, in receiving the information necessary to know and to understand their childhood and early development. On the other hand, it must be borne in mind that confidentiality of public records is of importance for receiving objective and reliable information, and that such confidentiality can also be necessary for the protection of third persons'.[25]

The Court considered that where legislation on access to files makes access dependent on the consent of the contributor, 'the interests of the individual seeking access to records relating to his private and family life must be secured when a contributor to the records either is not available or improperly refuses consent'. Such a system must provide an independent authority to decide finally whether access should be granted. The Court found that the procedures followed 'failed to secure respect for Mr Gaskin's private and family life as required by Article 8 of the Convention'. In a previous judgment, the court had decided that 'although the essential object of Article 8 is to protect the individual against arbitrary interference by the public authorities, there may in addition be positive obligations inherent in an effective 'respect' for family life'.[26] The Court decided that

Graham Gaskin 'may have suffered some emotional distress and anxiety by reason of the absence of any independent procedure', and awarded him £5,000 damages.

In its report on the Gaskin case, the European Human Rights Commission had stated that the right to respect for family life required under Article 8 of the Convention 'requires that everyone should be able to establish details of their identity as individual human beings and that in principle they should not be obstructed by the authorities from obtaining such very basic information without specific justification'. This should clearly apply to basic information about parentage (see also Article 8, page 28). The Commission stated:

> 'In the present case the applicant was taken into care at a very young age and subsequently had very little contact with his natural family, or continuity of care from a substitute family ... In these circumstances the file compiled and maintained by the local authority provides the only coherent record of the applicant's early childhood and formative years. Hence the Commission finds that the refusal to allow the applicant access to the file is an interference with his right to respect for his private life'.[27]

There are two clear implications of the Gaskin case for current legislation on files: the right to identity for many children implies some rights of *retrospective* access to files, not included in any of the current legislation. And the decision also implies that there must be a right of appeal to an impartial authority against any refusal of access; again, current legislation does not provide this right (although in some cases it would be possible to seek judicial review of an authority's action where access was refused unreasonably or illegally).

Separation from parents

Article 9

'1. States Parties shall ensure that a child shall not be separated from his or her parents against their will, except when competent authorities subject to judicial review determine, in accordance with applicable law and procedures, that such separation is necessary for the best interests of the child. Such determination may be necessary in a particular case such as one involving abuse or neglect of the child by the parents, or one where the parents are living separately and a decision must be made as to the child's place of residence.

2. In any proceedings pursuant to paragraph 1, all interested parties shall be given an opportunity to participate in the proceedings and make their views known.

3. States Parties shall respect the right of the child who is separated from one or both parents to maintain personal relations and direct contact with both parents on a regular basis, except if it is contrary to the child's best interests.

4. Where such separation results from any action initiated by a State Party, such as the detention, imprisonment, exile, deportation or death (including death arising from any cause while the person is in the custody of the State) of one or both parents or of the child, that State Party shall, upon request, provide the parents, the child or, if appropriate, another member of the family with the essential information concerning the whereabouts of the absent member(s) of the family unless the provision of the information would be detrimental to the well-being of the child. States Parties shall further ensure that the submission of such a request shall of itself entail no adverse consequences for the person(s) concerned.'

Article 9(1) and (2)

There are a number of ways in which the State may act to separate a child from his or her parents against their will. This article insists that such action can only be justified where it is 'necessary for the best interests of the child'. What of separation caused by the imprisonment of one or other parent (and in particular the significant number of cases in which imprisonment leads to the separation of mothers and babies)? Or separation caused by the deportation of one or both parents of a child who has a right to remain in the UK? At present proceedings which may lead to separation of a child from his or her parents may take place without consideration of the child's interests (see Article 3, page 9), and without any opportunity (as guaranteed by Article 9(2)) for the child and other interested parties to participate and make their views known.

Procedures for emergency protection of children under the Children Act 1989 due to come into effect in October 1991 appear to satisfy this article: the child, parent or certain other people have a right to apply for discharge of an emergency protection order after 72 hours if the order was made *ex parte*, and there is also the opportunity to challenge in court any request to extend an order beyond eight days. (But the current procedures for place of safety orders in England and Wales – up to October 1991 – breach the article by denying any judicial review, as do those in Northern Ireland. Legislation in Scotland, allowing for the child to be brought before a hearing and appeal to a sheriff, which may satisfy the article, is currently (June 1991) under review, as is legislation in Northern Ireland).

Under the Children Act, courts in England and Wales making decisions following separation must regard the child's welfare as the paramount consideration, and there is an obligation to ascertain and take account of the child's views.

Children's rights to participate in adoption proceedings are still limited: they cannot be parties except in proceedings in the High Court.

Wards of court have no right to 'participate' in High Court hearings and make their views known, in breach of Article 9(2), even though such proceedings may lead to separation from parents.

Fully implementing rights to participation implies providing rights to appropriate translations and interpreters throughout the procedures for children, parents and others whose first language is not English, or who have disabilities.

Article 9(3)

Article 9(3) makes a presumption of the child's right of access to both parents, unless to do so is 'contrary to the child's best interests'. In England and Wales, there is no such presumption under the

Children Act, except for children in care: under section 34(1) the local authority is obliged to allow the child in its care 'reasonable contact with parents', unless to do so is incompatible with safeguarding and promoting the child's welfare (it must also take reasonable steps to inform parents of a child's address, which is relevant to Article 9(4)). Otherwise, the right is subject to the court's power to decide access, with the child's welfare as its paramount consideration; the child's views must be ascertained and taken into account. In Scotland, there is a common law presumption of reasonable access to children in care, which the current Child Care Law Review recognises, but plans to clarify by setting out in statute.

The Children Act 1989 (S.23) does oblige local authorities looking after children in England and Wales to ensure, so far as is reasonable, practicable and consistent with the children's welfare, that they are placed near their home, and that if the authority is looking after siblings, they are accommodated together (see also Article 8, page 28). It should be emphasised that Article 9(3) only allows refusal of access where access is judged to be 'contrary to the child's best interests'. It appears that limitations on 'personal relations and direct contact' for children whose parents are detained in prison, or under immigration or mental health legislation, would breach this article, unless they could be justified by the 'best interests' of the children concerned.

Children placed in care or in an institution who have a disability and/or learning difficulty appear to suffer discrimination in relation to access to their parents, which also raises issues under Article 23: recent statistics from the Office of Population Censuses and Surveys (OPCS) suggested that 50 per cent of children with disabilities in residential care had no contact with parents or families. Contact appeared to vary substantially depending on which authority – health or social services or education – was looking after the children, and on the category of institution (poverty may be another reason – see page 86 for further discussion).

Contact between parents and children in many circumstances is limited by lack of resources: one example is access visits by non-custodial parents on income support. There is no allocation in income support awards for account to be taken of a non-custodial parent's responsibilities: the proposals in the White Paper, *Children Come First* (1991), and the Child Support Bill may well work counter to general moves towards shared care by making distinctions between absent parents and caring parents, and introducing a rigid formula for maintenance based on this distinction.[28]

Poverty is also a major reason for limiting parental contact and visits to children in institutions. The National Association for the Welfare of Children in Hospital (NAWCH) has reported that many families on low income, or receiving income support, have found it impossible to get help to pay the costs of visiting children in hospital, although this is known to be a vital factor for children's recovery and welfare. NAWCH found that over half the applications for grants to the Social Fund had been refused, although guidelines suggest that fares to visit a child in hospital should be given as a grant rather than a loan, and regarded as a priority need. Introduction of the Social Fund has undoubtedly made the situation far worse. Social services also have a power – but no duty – to pay such expenses. In the absence of legal duties, it becomes a matter of resources and thus discriminatory.

It is clear that current legislation and practice are denying many children rights to maintain personal relations and direct contact with their parents, in circumstances in which such contact might be particularly beneficial.

Article 9(4)

Where parents are imprisoned, or detained under immigration or mental health law, there is no legal obligation to inform children of the place of detention. Parents and children are not necessarily informed of the others' whereabouts when children are taken into care or into a place of safety: on occasions this may be justifiable in the interests of the child, but there should be a presumption that the information will be made available unless to do so threatens the best interests of the child.

Family reunification

Article 10

'1. In accordance with the obligation of States Parties under Article 9, paragraph 1, applications by a child or his or her parents to enter or leave a State Party for the purpose of family reunification shall be dealt with by States Parties in a positive, humane and expeditious manner. States Parties shall further ensure that the submission of such a request shall entail no adverse consequences for the applicants and for the members of their family.

2. A child whose parents reside in different States shall have the right to maintain on a regular basis save in exceptional circumstances personal relations and direct contacts with both parents. Towards that end and in accordance with the obligation of States Parties under Article 9, paragraph 2, States Parties shall respect the right of the child and his or her parents to leave any country, including their own, and to enter their own country. The right to leave any country shall be subject only to such restrictions as are prescribed by law and which are necessary to protect the national security, public order (*ordre public*), public health or morals or the rights and freedoms of others and are consistent with the other rights recognized in the present Convention.'

The rights guaranteed to the child under this article conflict with our existing immigration law (and the Government has indicated that in ratifying the Convention it is likely to enter a reservation because of this conflict (see page 181)). Current law does not provide for the welfare of the child to be considered at all, certainly not as a paramount or even primary consideration, when decisions about immigration, emigration, or deportation are being made.

Under this article together with Article 2, all children in the UK who have one or both parents living abroad should have equal rights to 'personal relations and direct contacts' on a regular basis with both parents (subject to the very limited conditions in Article 10(2)).

Family unity

Children's rights to join parents in the UK are limited under current law. They became even more limited with implementation of the Immigration Act 1988 and changes to the Immigration Rules. The Act removed the theoretically unqualified right to family unity in the UK, previously held by some British and other Commonwealth citizens who were settled in the UK before 1973. This means in effect that there is now a means test on all applications for family unity in the UK. The Act also gave the Home Office the power to charge fees for settlement, made 'overstaying' a continuing offence, and reduced appeal rights.

Unmarried children under 18 may be able to join their parents in the UK if both are settled, and if the immigration authorities are satisfied about their relationship. If one parent is dead, a child may join the other parent if settled here. But if only one parent is settled here, and the other is not, a child has no automatic right to join the parent. In those circumstances a child may be admitted for settlement only if the parent settled in the UK has had the 'sole responsibility' for the child's upbringing, or 'there are serious and compelling family or other considerations which make exclusion undesirable ... and suitable arrangements have been made for the child's care'. The operation of this aspect of the Immigration Rules is clearly in breach of this article. In operation it has discriminated in particular against children of Afro-Caribbean origin, because of family and migration patterns.

The report of a formal investigation by the Commission for Racial Equality (CRE) into immigration control procedures found:

> 'The rules governing the admission of children to join one parent in the United Kingdom raise fundamental problems of interpretation and administration. The concept of 'sole responsibility' is not clear-cut and simple ... A great deal of discretion was available to entry clearance officers.'[29]

The investigation found that instructions to entry clearance officers made a distinction between children aged under 12, who were normally to be admitted if arrangements for their care in the UK were satisfactory, and those over 12, for whom there needed to be special compassionate reasons for admission. The instructions continued:

'The compassionate considerations should arise in the country where the child lives and be exceptional in comparison with the ordinary circumstances of children there; it is not sufficient to show that the child would be better off in the United Kingdom. There must be evidence that the child is suffering from conditions in its own country which make the continuance of its current mode of life intolerable.'

Such instructions are very far indeed from making the child's best interests a 'primary consideration' (see Article 3, page 8).

It is policies such as these that the UK Government will be defending if it chooses to issue reservations to articles of the Convention because of current immigration law (see page 181). The CRE concluded that it could see no good reason why the rules should discriminate between children joining two parents in the UK and children joining one parent:

'When the application is for a child to live with a relative other than a parent, it is reasonable that admission should be conditional on exceptional circumstances. In such cases, in our view, the benefits to the child should be the paramount consideration, and it would be better if the rule was drafted to allow admission provided it was in the best interests of the child. The necessary judgments should be based on the advice of professional staff with appropriate training and qualifications.'

The Immigration Rules also discriminate against the right to family reunification of many adopted children. The Rules are designed to prevent settlement in the UK of children 'adopted for convenience'. As noted above in discussing the right to nationality guaranteed by Article 7 (see page 24), the British Nationality Act 1981 also discriminates against children adopted abroad in that if adopted abroad by British citizen parents, children do not gain British citizenship, as do children born abroad to most British citizen parents. They must apply for registration as British citizens at the discretion of the Home Secretary. The rights to enter the UK of children adopted abroad who are not British citizens are subject to a very restrictive test in the Immigration Rules – that 'there has been a genuine transfer of parental responsibility on the grounds of the original parents' inability to care for the child and the adoption is not one of convenience arranged to facilitate the child's admission'. Again, this is far from any consideration of the children's best interests.

The European Court of Human Rights accepted in a recent case that the denial of children's rights to family life under immigration law may breach the European Convention on Human Rights. While the State has a right to determine its own immigration laws, there must be a proper balance of the individual's and the State's interests. The case involved a divorced man's right to maintain contact with his daughter, although living separately from her: the father was living separately but frequently visiting, which in the eyes of the court amounted to 'family life', interfered with by the father's loss of his residence permit and subsequent deportation. The court emphasised that the interference was substantial because of the young child's need to have regular contact with her father.[30]

Recently another application concerning family reunion made by three children, British citizens, and their father, a Nigerian citizen with a history of illegal immigration to the UK, has been declared admissible by the European Commission in Strasbourg.[31] The children – twins aged eight and a five-year-old – were living with their mother when she was killed in a car accident in 1986. Their father tried to come to England, but was allowed only temporary admission and eventually sent back to Nigeria, despite strong representations that this was not in the children's interests. The children joined him but suffered great hardship. The application to the European Commission alleged breaches of two articles of the European Convention on Human Rights (see page 188): Article 3 (protection from inhuman or degrading treatment and punishment) and Article 8 (right to private and family life). In this case, as a consequence of the Commission's decision, the Home Office has agreed to pay for the three children and their father to return to Britain.[32]

Arrangements for considering requests for family reunification have been heavily criticised, and there is a great deal of evidence that applications are frequently not dealt with in a 'positive, humane and expeditious manner'. In particular, delays in handling applications from the Indian sub-continent discriminate against many children and young people on grounds of colour and ethnic origin. There is further discrimination against poor families and children: all applicants (except those from the European Community) must now satisfy the authorities that the family can be supported and accommodated in the UK without recourse to public funds.

DNA 'fingerprinting' now provides conclusive evidence of family relationships (the fee for settlement applications has been raised to £80 to cover the costs of these tests). Many young people, refused settlement in the UK because the immigration authorities did not believe the family relationships they claimed, have been able to prove the relationship through DNA testing. However, if they do so when they are over 18 (the upper age limit to qualify as a dependent child), there is no automatic right of settlement, although there have been limited concessions. The use of DNA tests raises the standard of proof, as well as introducing other issues of family privacy and confidentiality; the results are not necessarily conducive to children's welfare.

The right to family reunification of children admitted as refugees is severely restricted. Most unaccompanied refugee children (see also Article 22, page 82) are given exceptional leave to remain in the UK, rather than settled status, so that they have no right to family reunification in the UK at all. These children have often been traumatised by experience of war, violence and separation and may have endured extreme hardship in coming to the UK: limiting any possible family reunification contradicts their best interests, and ignores recommendations made by the United Nations High Commissioner for Refugees. In other cases refugee adults, given exceptional leave to remain, are not normally able to bring in children for four years.

The Immigration Act 1988 removed the right of appeal before removal in respect of those claiming to be British citizens on arrival in the UK, who may include children. The United Kingdom Immigrants' Advisory Service suggested in its annual report for 1987/88 that this 'erodes a fundamental principle of British justice that administrative action which affects an individual must be subject to independent review'.[33] Article 6 of the European Convention on Human Rights guarantees everyone (including children in the UK) 'a fair and public hearing by an independent and impartial tribunal' for the determination of their civil rights (see page 189). There is also no right of appeal, except on the facts of the decision, against deportation for people who have been in the UK less than seven years; such appeals cannot consider factors such as family and children. (This legislation also conflicts with Article 9 – the right of children not to be separated from parents except where 'competent authorities subject to judicial review' decide the separation is necessary for the best interests of the child: (see page 32).

In breach of Article 12 (see page 44) there is no obligation on those involved in any of the 'judicial and administrative proceedings' under immigration or nationality law in the UK to ascertain and give consideration to the views of affected children (nor any procedures for children to be supported with advocacy if on their own, as in the case of unaccompanied refugee children).

European Community law gives rights of family reunification to EC nationals working in another country. There is thus discrimination against children of non-EC national parents.

The UK cannot fully implement this article and others in the Convention without major changes in immigration law and procedure.

Illicit transfer and non-return of children

Article 11

'1. States Parties shall take measures to combat the illicit transfer and non-return of children abroad.

2. To this end, States Parties shall promote the conclusion of bilateral or multilateral agreements or accession to existing agreements.'

The law to combat child abduction has been significantly tightened throughout the UK in recent years. The Child Abduction Act 1984 makes abduction of children under 16 an offence; abductors can be extradited from those countries currently having extradition treaties with the UK (the equivalent legislation for Northern Ireland is the Child Abduction (NI) Order 1985). The Child Abduction and Custody Act 1985 gave force throughout the UK to two international conventions: the Hague Convention on the Civil Aspect of International Child Abduction, and the European Convention on the Recognition and Enforcement of Custody Decisions. As this article emphasises, it is only through international cooperation that child abduction can be effectively combated.

One concern about the two Conventions is that they do not give sufficient priority to the best interests of the child (contrary to Article 3 of the UN Convention (see page 8); the emphasis is on returning the child to the country from which he or she has been removed. And there are only limited obligations to ascertain and pay due regard to the child's wishes and feelings (contrary to Article 12 (see page 44).

Until implementation of the Family Law Reform Act 1986 it was possible for a person to remove a child from one part of the UK to another in order to evade a custody order. The Act made provision for the recognition and enforcement throughout the UK of custody orders made in any part of it. Before this provision comes into effect, the order must be registered in the new jurisdiction, or proceedings for enforcement taken there. The Act also provides that an order made in any part of the UK, prohibiting removal of a child from any part of the UK, shall be enforceable throughout the UK. The provisions of the Act can be extended to Dependent Territories by an Order in Council.

There have been proposals to improve procedures to safeguard abducted children, including appointing a 'Children's Commissioner' to represent the interests of abducted children in the UK and abroad and to provide necessary support, extending legal aid to cover necessary legal action abroad, and making abduction less easy where there are custody disputes by restrictions on passports.[34]

Under the Convention, all states have a duty to work towards implementation worldwide. So in the context of this article, and for the benefit of its own and the world's abducted children, the UK should exert pressure on countries which have not yet fully accepted the relevant international conventions.

Hearing the child's views

Article 12

'1. States Parties shall assure to the child who is capable of forming his or her own views the right to express those views freely in all matters affecting the child, the views of the child being given due weight in accordance with the age and maturity of the child.

2. For this purpose, the child shall in particular be provided the opportunity to be heard in any judicial and administrative proceedings affecting the child, either directly, or through a representative or an appropriate body, in a manner consistent with the procedural rules of national law.'

This article is the cornerstone of the Convention's insistence that children must not be treated as silent objects of concern, but as people with their own views and feelings which must be taken seriously.

Since implementation of the Children Act 1975, children in care in England and Wales have had the right to have their views ascertained and taken into consideration when decisions affecting them are being made, and there are similar duties in Scotland. Children in care in Northern Ireland have no statutory right to have their views ascertained and taken into consideration; the law is currently (June 1991) under review.

For England and Wales, the Children Act 1989 re-enacts and extends these rights to involvement in decision-making. In addition to authorities' duties to take account of the wishes and feelings of children they are looking after, and of other children in need, courts making decisions about children's upbringing must take account of the ascertainable wishes and feelings of the child. There are similar obligations on voluntary organisations caring for children, and on the proprietors of private (registered) children's homes. And when a police constable takes a child into police protection in an emergency, there is an obligation 'as soon as is reasonably practicable' to 'take such steps as are reasonably practicable to discover the wishes and feelings of the child' (Children Act, S. 46(3)). But, curiously, there is no matching duty to 'pay due consideration' to the child's wishes and feelings.) In Scotland a child removed in an emergency must be brought before a children's hearing on the first possible day, and at that stage his or her feelings should be ascertained and should have a distinct place in the proceedings. But there is currently concern that children's views have not been adequately considered, that children have not received appropriate information and advice, and that in some cases a decision has been made to dispense with children's presence at hearings.

Children's views at home

Currently parents or others exercising parental responsibility (with the exception of care authorities, as outlined above) have no obligation to ascertain or have regard to children's wishes before making decisions, even major ones, which affect the child. But, interestingly, the Scottish Law Commission, in a Discussion Paper published in October 1990, asked:

> 'Should it be provided that a person with parental rights, in reaching any major decision relating to the child in the exercise of those rights, must so far as practicable ascertain the wishes and feelings of the child regarding the decision and give due consideration to them, having regard to the child's age and understanding?'[35]

The Commission commented that it could see great attractions in the idea:

> 'It emphasises that the child is a person in his or her own right and that his or her views are entitled to respect and consideration... There could be value in a provision which established a duty to consult the child, even if it was vague and unenforceable. It could have an influence on behaviour.'

In Finland, the Child Custody and Right of Access Act 1983 states that before a parent who has custody:

> 'makes a decision on a matter relating to the person of the child, he or she shall, where possible, discuss the matter with the child taking into account the child's age and maturity and the nature of the matter. In making the decision the custodian shall give due consideration to the child's feelings, opinions and wishes.'

To implement Article 12 fully, similar legislation encouraging children's participation in major decisions at home should be implemented throughout the UK. If the Convention is to affect seriously the lives of children, its provisions must be known and respected not only by governments, authorities and institutions, but also by those living with children.

The childcare system has gone very much further, in particular in England and Wales under the Children Act 1989, to satisfy this article and take children's views seriously, and one may assume that Scottish and Northern Ireland childcare law will be similarly reformed.

But while the Children Act may place clear obligations on courts and authorities to ascertain and take account of children's wishes and feelings, the implications of the principle for practice are a long way from being accepted. For example, current (June 1991) guidance on case conferences about suspected child abuse, while encouraging involvement of parents, makes no mention of attendance or involvement by the child, which should surely be the primary consideration, and a necessary implication of Article 12. The obligation to ensure that the child has an opportunity to express views clearly and have them taken into account needs to be built into procedures from the earliest stage. Revised guidance issued in draft by the Department of Health for consultation (June 1991) does however suggest:

> 'Whenever children are old enough to express their wishes and feelings and to participate in the process of assessment, planning and review, arrangements should be made which allow them to attend the case conference.'

Education law

Other major services in which daily decisions profoundly affect children's lives are under no obligation to consult children or to encourage their participation. The education system, supposedly aimed at increasing individuals' ability to control their own lives, has a legislative framework which denies children and young people (up to the age of 18 in England, Wales and Northern Ireland and to the age of 16 in Scotland) any formal voice whatsoever. Reforms promoted as increasing 'consumer involvement' in education have assumed that parents rather than children and young people are the consumers, and have extended to parents rights of access to decision-making, appeal, and so on.

The obligation in Article 12(2) to provide an opportunity to hear children 'in any judicial and administrative proceedings' affecting them is clearly breached by the lack of any right to be heard, for example:

- in the procedures for choosing a school and school choice appeals; for children with special needs, in assessment and placement decisions, reviews, reassessments and appeals under the Education Act 1981 (and the equivalent legislation for Scotland and Northern Ireland);
- in the various formal administrative procedures under the National Curriculum and arrangements for excluding certain children from it;
- in the arrangements for appeal against school exclusions.

The one remarkable exception is that pupils under an 'education supervision order' (introduced by the Children Act for England and Wales) have a right to be consulted: before giving any directions the supervisor must ascertain the wishes and feelings of the child, including in particular wishes on where the child should be educated, and give them due consideration. It is significant that this provision was introduced in the context of a review of childcare law, not education legislation (Children Act, schedule 3, para 12(2) and (3).

The obligations placed by the Children Act on the proprietors of private children's homes, and on voluntary organisations, to consult children before making decisions, highlight the lack of any equivalent duty on those providing maintained and independent schools (and non-maintained special schools), and private health institutions (nursing homes and mental nursing homes).

In the health service, there is no legislative duty to consult children. Children and young people have rights (albeit still not consistently respected) to exercise control over their treatment. In Scotland, when children become 'minors' (12 for girls and 14 for boys) they gain a right to control their own medical treatment. In England and Wales, young people acquire a right to consent or withhold consent to medical treatment for themselves at 16 under the Family Law Reform Act 1969. Below that age the implications of the Gillick judgment are that children judged to have 'sufficient understanding and intelligence' are also entitled to make decisions for themselves.[36] But Article 12 implies the additional and general right of children – not written into health legislation – to express views as soon as they are capable of doing so, and to have those views taken seriously.

Similarly, children and young people have no right to be heard in hearings about immigration and nationality (see Article 10, page 36) or in criminal trials of their parents, or social security appeals, and so on. There is no right to be heard in the procedures which lead to children and young people being excluded from certain categories of film, set by the British Board of Film Censors, approved by the Home Office and accepted by local authorities.

The degree to which Article 12 is consistently implemented is of crucial importance to the status of children. It is a clearly worded article with very wide implications for law, policy and practice in the UK. Implementation implies the consistent extension of the principle of participation – seeking the ascertainable views of children and young people, and giving them due consideration having regard to age and understanding – beyond the Children Act to all relevant statutes for England and Wales, Scotland and Northern Ireland. To implement the article without discrimination also involves ensuring that participation is equally possible for children and young people whose first language is not English, through the provision of translations and interpreters, and in appropriate forms such as braille and signing, and with any necessary support, for children with disabilities and learning difficulties.

But the article also implies building the principle into local policy and practice, into the ethical codes of the professions which work with children and young people, and into the daily conduct of those who live with children and young people.

Freedom of expression

Article 13

'1. The child shall have the right to freedom of expression; this right shall include freedom to seek, receive and impart information and ideas of all kinds, regardless of frontiers, either orally, in writing or in print, in the form of art, or through any other media of the child's choice.

2. The exercise of this right may be subject to certain restrictions, but these shall only be such as are provided by law and are necessary:

(a) for respect of the rights or reputations of others; or

(b) for the protection of national security or of public order (*ordre public*), or of public health or morals.'

Article 10 of the European Convention on Human Rights (see page 188), guarantees freedom of expression with similar wording, but with the inclusion of 'freedom to hold opinions' as a basic right. This article of the UN Convention has obvious implications for parents' relationship with their children, and the degree of freedom allowed to the growing child (do parents or the child decide, for example, whether a child should be interviewed on radio or television, or take an active part in a public meeting?). Restrictions on freedom of expression may become more formal when the state is involved in parenting – for children in the care of the local authority and for wards of court. This article, taken in conjunction with Article 2, implies that these children should have equal freedom of expression. The insistence of the High Court on anonymity for wards, which is not dependent on the ward's own view, would appear to conflict with the article.

To implement Article 13 fully, the powers of local authority parents and the High Court in wardship should be limited by the principle of respecting the child's freedom of expression (subject to the limitations in Article 13 (2)(a) and (b)).

The education system should surely play a large part in promoting children's freedom of expression. A centrally drafted and enforced National Curriculum, imposed with no consultation of school students, substantially limits the ability of individual schools to promote this right in England and Wales. At a local level, the right (set out in the Education (No. 2) Act 1986, S.18) of a maintained school governing body in England and Wales to veto all sex education or control its content and delivery directly conflicts with children's right to receive information of a crucial kind (the Act also insists that where there is sex education, governing bodies and head teachers 'shall take such steps as are reasonably practicable to secure... that it is given in such a way as to encourage ... pupils to have due regard to moral considerations and the value of family life').

Section 28 of the Local Government Act 1988 prohibits the intentional promotion of homosexuality through publishing material or teaching by local authorities in England, Wales and Scotland. In particular, authorities are banned from promoting the teaching in any maintained school of the acceptability of homosexuality as a 'pretended family relationship'. Given that local authorities have no control over the sex education offered in schools, Section 28 is unlikely to have any significant effect on its content (there is some evidence that it may have influenced choice of plays, for example, for pupils to attend on outings, leading to discrimination against gay and lesbian theatre groups). But the generally discriminatory nature of Section 28 may prejudice the freedom of expression of lesbian and gay young people, and their rights to 'appropriate' information under Article 17 (see page 62)

In addition, the discriminatory age of consent for consensual homosexual activity (referred to on page 3) potentially denies freedom of expression to gay young men aged under 21.

The Education (No. 2) Act 1986 Act directly limits the right to freedom of expression of younger pupils in maintained schools in England and Wales, giving local education authorities, governing bodies and head teachers a duty (under S.44) to forbid 'the pursuit of partisan political activities by any of those registered pupils at the school who are junior pupils; and ... the promotion of partisan political views in the teaching of any subject in the school'. Section 45 of the Act obliges local education authorities' governing bodies and head teachers to 'take such steps as are reasonably practicable' to ensure that when political issues are brought to the attention of pupils at the school, or when they are taking part in extra-curricular activities provided or organised for pupils at the school, 'they are offered a balanced presentation of opposing views'. Such limitations on what is provided for pupils within the curriculum may limit their freedom to express views on controversial subjects in school.

These limitations do not apply in Scotland.

Children's rights to freedom of expression through art and other media, such as music, may be drastically limited by resource variations between local education authorities (see Article 31, page 121).

School uniform

Another issue concerning freedom of expression over which there is frequent conflict between schools and pupils and their parents is that of school uniform and other matters of personal appearance (such as hair length, the wearing of jewellery, and the wearing of political and other badges.) The courts have supported heads who impose a strict dress code (and even heads who refuse to allow girls to wear trousers in school); such limitations on freedom of expression are sometimes also extended to school staff. The grounds for restricting children's freedom of expression given in Article 13(2) would not appear to justify the limitations currently imposed by many schools (and by some other institutions such as children's homes).

So far, the European human rights machinery has not backed school students' right to freedom of expression in their choice of clothing: a mother's application alleging that a school's uniform rules breached her and her son's rights under the Human Rights Convention was rejected. The European Commission of Human Rights found that:

> 'although the right to freedom of expression may include the right of a person to express his ideas through the way he dresses, it has not been established on the facts of the case that the applicant's children have been prevented from expressing a particular opinion or idea by means of their clothing.'[37]

But this decision would appear to leave open the possibility of a successful application where, for instance, a head teacher forbade a pupil from wearing a CND badge in school. A celebrated decision of the United States Supreme Court – the Tinker case – upholding school students' rights to wear black arm bands in protest at US involvement in Vietnam, stated: 'It can hardly be argued that either students or teachers lose their constitutional rights to freedom of speech or expression at the schoolhouse gate'.[38]

In certain cases, restrictions on dress and appearance may breach the Race Relations Act 1976. In 1983, an orthodox Sikh boy, suing via his father, established that refusing him admission to a school unless he removed his turban and cut his hair amounted to unlawful discrimination under the Act.[39]

And it seems likely that dress codes, imposed as a condition of entry to a school, which discriminate on grounds of sex (forbidding girls from wearing trousers for example) would be found to breach the Sex Discrimination Act; they may also breach this article of the Convention, taken in conjunction with Article 2.

Freedom of thought, conscience and religion

Article 14

'1. States Parties shall respect the right of the child to freedom of thought, conscience and religion.

2. States Parties shall respect the rights and duties of the parents and, when applicable, legal guardians, to provide direction to the child in the exercise of his or her right in a manner consistent with the evolving capacities of the child.

3. Freedom to manifest one's religion or belief may be subject only to such limitations as are prescribed by law and are necessary to protect public safety, order, health or morals or the protection of the rights and freedoms of others.'

The European Human Rights Convention has a similar but more strongly worded guarantee of this fundamental right, which applies equally to children. Article 9 states:

'Everyone has the right to fredom of thought, conscience and religion; this right includes freedom to change his religion or belief and freedom, either alone or in community with others, and in public or private, to manifest his religion or belief, in worship, teaching, practice and observance.'

It is clear that some parents currently do impose religion on their children, forcing attendance and involvement in religious ceremonies and practices. There is no confirmation of the basic rights guaranteed by this article in statute, which it would appear to require. In Scotland, 'minor' children have a right to choose their own religion (at the age of 12 for girls and 14 for boys, thus involving discrimination in breach of Article 2 against boys).[40]

A child in care in England and Wales must not be brought up 'in any religious persuasion other than that in which he would have been brought up if the order had not been made' (Children Act, S. 33(6)). This means that the right of a child in care to be converted to a particular religion different from that of his or her upbringing and, for example be fostered with a family of that religion is denied. And since this is a statutory duty of local authorities, it overrides consideration of the child's wishes. A draft of new regulations due to be implemented in October 1991 under the Children Act 1989 to apply to children's homes states:

> 'The responsible authority shall ensure that each child accommodated in each children's home is enabled, so far as practicable, to attend the services of, and to receive instruction in, and to observe any requirement (whether as to dress, diet or otherwise) of the religious persuasion to which he belongs'.

The Christian ethos of many voluntary childcare organisations providing accommodation for children in care may raise issues under this article.

The implication of the Gillick decision is that if children have 'sufficient understanding and intelligence' they have a right to make their own decisions about religion, independent of their parents.[41] And, under the Children Act (S.8), a child has the right to apply to court for an order to vary aspects of his or her upbringing. (Children in care under a care order do not have the right to make Section 8 applications.) It is up to the court to decide whether or not to hear such applications. But parents could also seek a Section 8 order if they thought a particular religion chosen by a child was harmful. (It is also probably possible for a child in Scotland to apply for an order under Section 3 of the Law Reform (Parent and Child) (Scotland) Act 1986, relating to any exercise of parental rights.)

Wards of court have no right to freedom of religion, in that all major decisions must be referred to the High Court.

In education law, parents have a right to withdraw their children from religious worship and education in schools, and can ask for special lessons in a particular religion. But children do not have these rights.

This article, read in conjunction with Article 2, challenges the current discrimination whereby certain established religious groups gain funding for voluntary aided school status, while others do not. There are many voluntary-aided Church of England and Catholic and some Jewish schools; but applications from, for example, groups of Muslim parents have failed. The special status of voluntary aided and controlled schools appears to give children from established faiths the right to pursue their religion in an appropriate school setting – a right which children of other faiths do not have. The

Swann Report, *Education for All*, on the education of minority ethnic children recommended that it was time to reconsider the role of the Church in education and the legal provisions in the 1944 Act on religion in schools.[42]

The Education Reform Act 1988 re-enacted and in certain ways changed the provisions on religious education and worship in schools in England and Wales so that, for example, (S. 7) the collective worship required in county (fully maintained) schools 'shall be wholly or mainly of a broadly Christian character [reflecting] the broad traditions of Christian belief without being distinctive of any particular Christian denomination'. The section allows relevant circumstances relating to the family backgrounds of pupils and their ages and aptitudes to be taken into account. Nevertheless, it would appear to amount to further discrimination against children from religions other than Christianity. (In Scottish law there is no bias towards education of a Christian character.)

Freedom of association

Article 15

'1. States Parties recognize the right of the child to freedom of association and to freedom of peaceful assembly.

2. No restrictions may be placed on the exercise of these rights other than those imposed in conformity with the law and which are necessary in a democratic society in the interests of national security or public safety, public order (*ordre public*), the protection of public health or morals or the protection of the rights and freedoms of others.'

This article mirrors a similar one, Article 11, in the European Convention on Human Rights (but that article also specifically guarantees everyone 'the right to form and to join trade unions for the protection of his interests': in the UK it appears that most unions allow young people to join at 16, and some allow younger members).

Implementation of the Public Order Act 1986 introduced new restrictions on marches and assemblies, and a new offence of 'disorderly conduct'. It contains no positive right to take part in peaceful assembly and protest. Many commentators believed it put unacceptable limits on basic rights like those guaranteed under this article, and that in relation to young people in particular, the new offence of 'disorderly conduct' could bring them into further unconstructive conflict with the police.

Parents' control over their children's involvement in, for example, public meetings or peaceful demonstrations should be limited by the implications of the Gillick decision that once children are judged to have 'sufficient understanding and intelligence', they should be enabled to make decisions on important matters for themselves.[43] In institutions, and particularly in schools, children's rights to freedom of association, and to form and attend meetings, are certainly on occasion limited; none of the justifications for such limitations given in Article 15(2) normally applies. In the 1970s, the National Union of School Students had difficulty organising and recruiting members in some areas, because head teachers proscribed the organisation. Some headteachers have refused to allow CND branches to be formed, and meetings to be held, in schools. Similarly, the National Association of Young People in Care (NAYPIC) has had difficulty organising in some local authority areas.

The rights guaranteed under Article 15 are perhaps particularly important for children and young people in residential institutions, including boarding schools and children's homes.

It is common practice for shops to put up notices saying, for example: 'Only one child allowed in shop at one time', or even 'No unaccompanied children allowed'. Such actions discriminate against children's rights to freedom of association. Their justification – usually to prevent shoplifting by children – is weak; why discriminate in particular against children, and why not rely on other methods of crime prevention?

This article, read in conjunction with Article 2, raises the issue of the rights of children with disabilities and learning difficulties to freedom of association with other children. Schools, children's homes and private and NHS health institutions which segregate on grounds of disability may be unreasonably limiting this freedom (see Article 23, page 85). Language units may be segregating children on grounds of language and probably additionally on grounds of race, colour and ethnic origin.

The Children Act 1989 does, however, promote positive principles for local authorities providing services for children with disabilities: they must be designed 'to minimise the effect on disabled children within their area of their disabilities; and give such children the opportunity to lead lives which are as normal as possible' (Children Act 1989 schedule 2, para. 6).

Protection of privacy

Article 16

'1. No child shall be subjected to arbitrary or unlawful interference with his or her privacy, family, home or correspondence, nor to unlawful attacks on his or her honour and reputation.

2. The child has the right to the protection of the law against such interference or attacks.'

The European Convention on Human Rights (Article 8) reads: 'Everyone has the right to respect for his private and family life, his home and his correspondence.'

Children's rights to privacy are important whether they live at 'home' or spend significant periods of their lives in institutions. In considering children's rights to an 'adequate' standard of living, under Article 27 (see page 105), it is important to consider privacy: do children living with their parent(s) in one room in 'bed and breakfast' accommodation have sufficient privacy? At what age or stage should children have the right to their own private space, their own room? Most children's privacy is controlled by their parents, and by levels of family poverty or affluence. The principle of this article should be considered.

In institutions, children's right to privacy can be severely curtailed, and currently legislation does little to protect this right for children. A comprehensive review of legislation controlling all institutions used by children and young people should take account of the rights guaranteed by this article.

The Children Act provides relevant safeguards for some institutions in England and Wales: regulations due to apply to children's homes from October 1991 insist that there are facilities for children to meet parents and others privately, and a pay telephone available in a setting 'where it is possible to make and receive telephone calls in privacy'. The regulations on sanctions also insist that there must not be any restriction on or refusal to allow a child visits and communication (by letter and telephone) with parents, friends and other defined people, unless such limits are judged to be in the child's best interests.

The right to private correspondence (including telephone calls) is not guaranteed in all institutions for children and young people; where correspondence is opened on the grounds of safety or security (for example, searching for drugs or other forbidden articles) this should be done in front of the child, without reading the correspondence.

Children who live, sometimes for 52 weeks a year, in schools and health institutions do not in most cases have any such formal protection of their privacy (independent schools in England and Wales accommodating less than 50 children will be obliged under the Children Act 1989 to register as children's homes, and thus be covered by the detailed safeguards referred to above). In some settings – wards in long stay mental hospitals, dormitories of some boarding schools, shared cells in young offender institutions and prisons (see also Article 37, page 134) – there may be no privacy whatsoever. In certain cases in some children's homes, including secure accommodation and health units, closed circuit video cameras and two-way mirror screens are used to observe children – not necessarily with their knowledge, let alone their agreement – in bedrooms and other areas.

Sometimes residential institutions (run by social services, health and education departments), and some day schools and centres remove doors or door locks from toilets, and have only communal bathing and showering facilities. Young women may have their periods monitored by staff. Regulations applying to maintained school premises do at least insist on provision for storing pupils' belongings, and on space for 'private study and social purposes' for those aged 16 and over. Guidance for the implementation of the provisions of the Children Act 1989, aiming to ensure promotion of the welfare of children accommodated in independent boarding schools, draws attention to the need for lockable cupboards for children's personal belongings. It also says that boarders need to be able to

'enjoy a degree of privacy, when they can be alone, withdraw in pairs or small groups from the hurley-burley of communal life, to read, talk, be quiet, do nothing, withdraw from younger/older peers... [and] have access to appropriate staff in private.'

This article, read in conjunction with Article 2, emphasises that the fact that a child is in care, or living in an institution, or has disabilities or learning difficulties should not lead to any diminution in his or her right to privacy.

Teachers and others may unintentionally invade a child's privacy by, for example, requesting an essay on aspects of their home life, or for a child in care, insisting on building up a home 'profile'.

Children's and young people's right to control access by other people, including parents and professionals, to personal files stored by institutions, local authorities, and the like, needs to be reviewed in the light of this article and the similar article in the European Convention on Human Rights (see also Article 8, page 28). Current legislation does give children certain rights to control others', including parents', access to their social services file (Access to Personal Files (Social Services) Regulations 1989). But in education, children and young people themselves have no control over who sees their file – they are only given a right of access themselves at 16, and parents' rights of access continue until the pupil is 18 (for discussion of rights of access to files as part of a child's 'identity' see also Article 8, page 29).

Regulations place some limits on disclosure of school records (Education (School Records) Regulations 1989) and statements of special educational needs (Education (Special Educational Needs) Regulations 1983); there are similar limits in Scottish legislation. Limits on disclosure of records kept on computer are covered in the Data Protection Act 1984.

Guidance issued under the Children Act 1989 for England and Wales on records to be kept on children living in a children's home emphasise that they should be kept securely to ensure confidentiality.

Providing confidential references about children and young people – for example, for jobs, or for the Universities' Central Council on Admissions procedure for seeking a university place – has raised concerns because the subject has no right to check or challenge the information in them, and disclosure of it may breach privacy without the consent of the subject.

The use, without full agreement, of biographical details and photographs of a child in advertisements for foster parents or adoptive parents also breaches a child's right to privacy.

The law on libel and slander is equally available to a child or young person, who could take action through an adult 'next friend', but the absence of legal aid for such actions would pose a major hindrance. Attacks on children's and young people's 'honour or reputation' are not unknown in the tabloid press; for example, the *Sun* pilloried with gross inaccuracy a little boy under the headline 'THE WORST BRAT IN BRITAIN' in July 1989. But in May 1991 the boy, Jonathan Hunt, made legal history by becoming the first child in the UK to sue for defamation, and the *Sun* agreed in the High Court to pay substantial libel damages.[44]

Access to appropriate information

Article 17

'States Parties recognize the important functions performed by the mass media and shall ensure that the child has access to information and material from a diversity of national and international sources, especially those aimed at the promotion of his or her social, spiritual and moral well-being and physical and mental health. To this end, States Parties shall:

(a) Encourage the mass media to disseminate information of social and cultural benefit to the child and in accordance with the spirit of Article 29;

(b) Encourage international co-operation in the production, exchange and dissemination of such information and material from a diversity of cultural, national and international sources;

(c) Encourage the production and dissemination of children's books;

(d) Encourage the mass media to have particular regard to the linguistic needs of the child who belongs to a minority group or who is indigenous;

(e) Encourage the development of appropriate guidelines for the protection of the child from information and material injurious to his or her well-being bearing in mind the provisions of Articles 13 and 18.'

Here is a general standard against which to test the current diversity of the media, and in particular those newspapers, magazines and programmes aimed specifically at children and young people. The article implies not just monitoring but positive encouragement from government. To what extent, for example, does the new Broadcasting Act 1989, which controls independent radio and television, or the charter of the BBC reflect these particular concerns for children's rights and needs? What action has the Government taken to encourage newspapers and magazines to disseminate material of social and cultural benefit to children? The Government offers no particular incentive to those involved in publishing and disseminating children's books, and cutbacks in public expenditure have led to reductions in public library services for children, and in schools' ability to buy books. Are there sufficient obligations to meet the linguistic needs of minorities, not only minority ethnic groups but also deaf and blind children and young people, by, for example, ensuring the availability of material in appropriate forms and translations.

The final paragraph on protection of the child from injurious information and material must be considered in conjunction with the articles guaranteeing the child freedom of expression, and recognising parents' responsibilities for the upbringing and development of the child (Articles 13, page 49, and 18, page 64). In recent years there has been legislation to protect children from video nasties. There is a delicate balance to be achieved between necessary protection and unconstructive censorship.

Article 10(1) of the European Convention on Human Rights states:

> 'Everyone has the right to freedom of expression. This right shall include freedom to hold opinions and to receive and impart information and ideas without interference by public authority and regardless of frontiers'.

The right to 'receive information' (subject to limitations set out in Article 10(2), see page 191) has been held to include access to relevant personal files, which for children remains restricted, in particular in education (see also Article 8, page 30). The European Court of Human Rights has held that

> 'the right to freedom to receive information basically prohibits a Government from restricting a person from receiving information that others wish or may be willing to impart to him'.[45]

Parental responsibilities

Article 18

'1. States Parties shall use their best efforts to ensure recognition of the principle that both parents have common responsibilities for the upbringing and development of the child. Parents or, as the case may be, legal guardians, have the primary responsibility for the upbringing and development of the child. The best interests of the child will be their basic concern.

2. For the purpose of guaranteeing and promoting the rights set forth in this Convention, States Parties shall render appropriate assistance to parents and legal guardians in the performance of their child-rearing responsibilities and shall ensure the development of institutions, facilities and services for the care of children.

3. States Parties shall take all appropriate measures to ensure that children of working parents have the right to benefit from child care services and facilities for which they are eligible.'

Where parents are married, the principle of common responsibilities is accepted; where they are not, the Children Act 1989 for England and Wales allows non-marital fathers to acquire equal responsibilities, with the agreement of the mother or by order of the court. The Act introduces the concept of 'parental responsibilities' to replace the common law concept of 'parental rights'. The Gillick decision had already indicated that parents have no absolute rights over their children: what rights they have derive from their responsibilities to promote their children's welfare. The Scottish Law Commission, in a recent Discussion Paper on parents' rights and responsibilities, proposes that this principle should be written into a new statute.[46] It is not in the Children Act 1989 for England and Wales.

Where there is a dispute about upbringing, the Children Act sets out the court's duties to make decisions. In doing so, the welfare of the child is the paramount consideration. There is at present no obligation in statute that parents' basic concern for their children should be the children's best interests, as set down in the last sentence of Article 18(1). Local authority 'parents' for children in care are governed by such an obligation, and in common law the Gillick decision states a similar obligation.

The second and third paragraphs of the Article set out the general principle of state support for parenting, and for working parents in particular. They are couched in vague terms, but few would judge the existing levels of support in the UK to be adequate from the child's or parent's perspective.

While there is limited protection for women from dismissal related to pregnancy, there is no statutory provision for maternity leave for all women. Statutory maternity pay is very limited (in comparison with many European countries). Adoptive parents have no statutory entitlement to leave or benefits (raising an issue of discrimination under Article 2). There is no statutory provision of paternity leave in the UK – clearly breaching the spirit of this article. There is no statutory provision whatsoever of parental or family leave to enable parents to carry out their childrearing responsibilities. In some cases women are allowed extended maternity leave, but very few employers allow paid leave for such purposes as looking after a sick child, or looking for appropriate day care facilities or schools. The UK Government has been responsible for delaying implementation of the European Commission Directive on Parental Leave.[47]

Child benefit – a unique benefit, not means-tested and paid direct to the main carer – has fallen significantly in real value in recent years. It bears no relationship to the real cost of a child. Levels of family benefits, and the introduction of the cash-limited Social Fund, have increased family poverty (see page 105). Homelessness affects many families with children. And (with reference to Article 2) there is evidence that families from certain ethnic groups are disproportionately likely to suffer poverty and homelessness.

Families with a child with a disability or learning difficulty often have additional expenses which are not necessarily covered by benefit. The recent OPCS survey of disability suggests that further attention should be given to family support to avoid discrimination against these children. The survey found that families with a disabled child were more likely to be one-parent families and more likely to have two or more dependent children. On two other economic indicators these families compared less favourably with the general population: they had a lower rate of owner occupation (52 per cent compared with 65 per cent) and parents had lower employment rates (75 per cent of fathers were in employment compared with 89 per cent in the general population). Earnings of fathers and mothers were also on average less than the general population. One third of the families were receiving a benefit, one fifth a disability cost allowance. The survey found that on average the families were spending an additional £6.54 per week because of their child's disability. Families with disabled children had, on average, lower equivalent incomes than families in the general population, so when the extra costs are taken into account, these families have lower equivalent resources available to spend on other things. Twenty-eight per cent of families with a disabled child had less than half the average to spend.[48]

The built environment and transport facilities are unsympathetic to the needs of carers with children. Government – local and national – has in general done very little to 'encourage', in the words of Article 18, the development of 'institutions, facilities and services' for the care of children. The 'We Welcome Small Children' campaign has highlighted ways in which shops, restaurants, buses and trains could be designed to make life easier for childcarers.[49] Few shops provide childcare facilities – crèches and play areas, access for double and single buggies, changing and feeding facilities; and supermarkets still almost invariably stack sweets by checkouts, which adds to the stress of shopping for many families.

To fulfil the spirit of this Article, there should be legislation and guidelines for all relevant services – whether provided by central or local government, voluntary or private bodies – to protect the needs of carers.

With reference to Article 18(3), in comparison with other European countries, the UK has very low levels of publicly funded day care for children under three (2 per cent, compared with 20 per cent in France and Belgium and 48 per cent in Denmark). It also has the lowest level of publicly funded care and education for children between three and school starting age (44 per cent, compared with between 60 and 90 per cent in almost all other EC countries).[50]

The proportion of UK mothers in paid employment with a child under five has increased significantly from 29 per cent in 1985 to 37 per cent in 1988. The rate of full-time employment among single mothers is the lowest in the European Community (6 per cent in 1988) mainly because there is so little affordable local authority day care. Day nurseries provide for under 1 per cent of under-fives in

England, 0.5 per cent in Northern Ireland and just 0.14 per cent in
Wales, and these figures are falling (there are 34,000 places for 3.7
million under-fives in England, Wales and Scotland). In England in
1989 there was a lower proportion of under-fives in local authority
day nurseries than in 1985; a number of authorities in England and
Wales make no provision at all. There has been an increase in
availability of childminders however (places for almost 6 per cent of
under-fives in England, 4 per cent in Wales, 3.7 per cent in Scotland,
and just over 6 per cent in Northern Ireland, where there has been a
sharp increase), and a considerable increase in the numbers of
private nurseries.

There is heavy dependence on the voluntary sector, with part-time
places for about a third of children aged three to five. Twenty-five per
cent of three and four-year-olds in England, Wales and Scotland, are
in nursery schools or classes (37 per cent in Wales and 33 per cent in
Scotland as against 23 per cent in England). Twenty per cent of three
and four-year-olds are in infants' classes in primary schools.[51] In
Northern Ireland, compulsory school now starts for most children at
the age of four – this raises other issues (see page 121).

Variations in the availability of good quality day care discriminate
between children living in different regions of the UK. Data on the
ethnic background of users of day care services should be collected,
monitored and evaluated to ensure that no racial group is being
treated less favourably then others. Research suggests that mothers
of certain minority ethnic backgrounds have more children under
eight, and are also earning less while working longer and more
unsocial hours: this suggests a disproportionate need for good
quality day care. If day care is to be appropriate for all children, there
is a need to monitor and evaluate the procedures for registration and
staffing.

In 1990 the National Children's Bureau Under Fives Unit
published, in collaboration with statutory and voluntary under-fives
organisations, *A Policy for Young Children: – a Framework for Action*
which sets out targets and also principles which emphasise the value
to children of 'good quality pre-school experiences that are appropriate to their stage of development'.[52]

The Children Act 1989 gives local authorities in England and
Wales a duty to provide 'such daycare ... as is appropriate' for
'children in need' in their area who are under five and not attending
school (while other provisions on day care in the Children Act apply

to Scotland too, this duty does not: in Scotland the Child Care Law Review has not proposed identifying children in need; general social welfare duties will apply to all children, but it appears there will be no duty to provide day care). Authorities also have a duty to review day care provision in their area. Such reviews should pay particular attention to any discrimination in the provision of day care.

Protection from abuse and neglect

Article 19

'1. States Parties shall take all appropriate legislative, administrative, social and educational measures to protect the child from all forms of physical or mental violence, injury or abuse, neglect or negligent treatment, maltreatment or exploitation including sexual abuse, while in the care of parent(s), legal guardian(s), or any other person who has the care of the child.

2. Such protective measures should, as appropriate, include effective procedures for the establishment of social programmes to provide necessary support for the child and for those who have the care of the child, as well as for other forms of prevention and for identification, reporting, referral, investigation, treatment, and follow-up of instances of child maltreatment described heretofore, and, as appropriate, for judicial involvement.'

In the UK, public and governmental concern over child abuse, and in particular over child sexual abuse within the family, has mounted in recent years. The Cleveland affair led to a judicial inquiry, and in her report Lord Justice Butler-Sloss prefaced her recommendations on children with the declaration: 'The child is a person, not an object of concern'.[53] The relevant government departments produced new official guidance on child protection, and when the Children Act 1989 is implemented fully in October 1991, a revised legislative framework for emergency protection of children comes into effect. (The relevant law in Scotland and Northern Ireland is also currently (June 1991) under review.) Criminal law protects children from physical cruelty (except for what the law terms 'reasonable' physical punishment – see below) and also from sexual abuse. Recent changes in legislation have attempted to aid prosecution of abusers by improving the position of children giving evidence, and courts' attitude to their evidence (further changes are included in a Criminal Justice Bill currently (June 1991) before Parliament).

The Criminal Justice Bill proposes significant changes to make it easier for children's acccounts of sexual abuse or violence they have suffered to be brought before the court. The central reform is to allow children to give their evidence by means of a video-recording made soon after the abuse came to light. This recording will be shown to the court, but only in those cases where the child is available for cross examination via a TV link. This will protect the child from being in the same room as the alleged abuser and it is to be hoped that judges clamp down on aggressive questioning by barristers aimed at confusing and upsetting the child.

Those concerned with child protection remain far from satisfied that existing law, procedures and practice do enough to safeguard children. Child death inquiry reports have in many cases found a failure by those professionals involved to concentrate sufficiently on the interests of the child concerned, or to listen to and believe the child; there have also been frequent breakdowns in communication between different professionals.

Abuse is an extreme demonstration of the anti-child attitudes that still abound in the UK; the Government could take appropriate educational measures to encourage positive child friendly attitudes.

Department of Health statistics suggest that at 31 March 1990 there were approximately 43,900 children and young people on Child Protection Registers in England. This is a rate of 4.0 children per thousand in the population aged under 18. It also represents a 7 per cent increase over the previous year. During the year to 31 March 1990 about 26,800 children's names were added to Child Protection Registers in England, a rate of 2.5 children per thousand of the population under 18. This represented a 17 per cent increase over the previous year's registration. The largest group of registrations were for 'grave concern' (45%), followed by physical abuse (26%), sexual abuse (15%), neglect (13%) and emotional abuse (4%). Girls were more likely to be registered than boys and the youngest age group, under one year, the most vulnerable.[54]

The experience of ChildLine, the free national helpline for children launched in October 1986, provides a further demonstration of how many children are still suffering. In its first two years it counselled more than 47,000 children. The largest single issue children phone about is sexual abuse; the other two most common categories are physical abuse and problems relating to parents – divorce, witnessing parental fights, and alcohol or drug abuse. More than half the children who phone ChildLine about sexual abuse have never told anyone else: clearly current services whose aim is actively to support and help children are not perceived as accessible by the children.[55] Another recent report (see page 121) described how children's freedom of movement has suffered because of parents' fears of 'molestation' or accident.[56]

Lack of resources clearly limits the effectiveness of services against abuse: in a number of local areas social services departments have indicated that they have children on their 'child protection' registers who have no social worker allocated to them. In 1990, a report from the London Region of the Social Services Inspectorate revealed that 820 children on registers were unallocated (the previous year's figure was 600).[57] Recent child death inquiry reports have suggested that limited resources increase risks for children. For example, the report on the death of three-year-old Stephanie Fox in London in 1989 said: 'We believe that some aspects of the resource constraints adversely affected the ways in which Stephanie's case was conducted'.[58]

The call in this article for appropriate programmes to provide positive support for children and for families links it with Articles 26 and 27 (see pages 101 and 105) on rights to social security and children's standard of living, emphasising the need for the state to take positive measures to reduce the stress of parenting that in some cases leads to abuse. Much of the emphasis in recent and current reforms of legislation has been on emergency intervention, and on prosecution of abusers. This article suggests that what is needed is a much wider review of the causes of all forms of abuse of children, and consideration of methods of prevention. The National Society for the Prevention of Cruelty to Children has recently proposed that there should be a nationally coordinated programme for prevention of child abuse, aimed at adults and children, with child protection training for all those working with children; treatment programmes should be available to all victims of abuse, their families, and to abusers.

But the article does more than provide protection from severe child abuse by parents and other carers. It insists that children must be protected from 'all forms' of physical and mental violence. All adult citizens of the UK are protected by criminal law from assault, however minor. But in the case of children the law defends physical punishment. Parents and other carers currently have a common law freedom to use 'reasonable chastisement', and this is confirmed in statute in the Children and Young Persons Act 1933 (for England and Wales; there are similar provisions in legislation applying to

Scotland and Northern Ireland). The provision which makes cruelty a criminal offence specifically excludes physical punishment. Parental physical punishment is extremely common in the UK: recent research found almost two-thirds of a large sample of mothers admitting to smacking their babies before the age of one; almost all four-year-olds were being smacked, 7 per cent more than once a day, and a further two-thirds more than once a week; 22 per cent of seven-year-olds had already been hit with an implement.[59]

The current social and legal acceptance of hitting children is perhaps the most symbolic indication of their low status in our society. Five European countries have prohibited all physical punishment of children (Sweden in 1979; Finland in 1984; Denmark in 1986; Norway in 1987 and Austria in 1989). A recommendation of the Council of Europe Committee of Ministers in 1985 urged member states, including the UK, to 'review their legislation on the power to punish children in order to limit or indeed prohibit corporal punishment, even if violation of such a prohibition does not necessarily entail a criminal penalty'.[60]

Until the UK follows this recommendation and the example of the five countries, it will be in breach of the full implications of this article. In some countries, legal reforms have gone further than banning smacking and cover humiliating treatment of children too; in Sweden, for example, the Parenthood and Guardianship Code states: 'Children are entitled to care, security and a good upbringing. Children are to be treated with respect for their person and individuality and may not be subjected to corporal punishment or any other humiliating treatment'.

There is no equivalent to this positive statement of children's basic rights, even in the new Children Act for England and Wales. Such clear confirmation of the need for respect for the bodily integrity of the child should be added to our legislation. While it is assumed in relation to sexual abuse that a child must have the right to say 'no', there is no such right in relation to physical punishment – a gross invasion of the child's physical integrity. There is progress on this issue – many major child welfare and professional groups in the UK now support the campaign 'EPOCH – End Physical Punishment of Children'.[61] Most recently in October 1990, the Scottish Law Commission issued a discussion paper on parents' rights and responsibilities which seeks views on whether Scottish parents should lose their right to smack.[62]

Other articles of the Convention are also relevant to the protection of children and young people from physical punishment and other humiliating and degrading treatment outside the home: Article 28 insists that school discipline must be administered 'in a manner consistent with the child's human dignity and in conformity with the present Convention' (page 112); and Article 37 states that: 'No child shall be subjected to torture or other cruel, inhuman or degrading treatment or punishment' (page 134).

Outside the family home, there has been considerable progress in ending physical punishment of children, although in most cases the prohibitions do not in addition cover other undesirable sanctions. Throughout the UK, legislation has outlawed physical punishment in all state-supported education (the legislation does not protect pupils paid for by parents in independent schools – see page 135). Those in the various categories of children's home in England and Wales will all be protected when the Children Act is fully implemented in October 1991. Currently (June 1991) regulations covering local authority and voluntary children's homes prohibit 'any form of corporal punishment', and (with carefully defined exceptions in certain circumstances) other undesirable sanctions, including: any deprivation of food or drink; any restriction on the child's contact (both visits and communication by letter and phone) with parents, relatives and friends and certain other people; any requirement to wear distinctive or inappropriate clothing (placing children in pyjamas during the daytime has been a fairly common sanction in some homes); the use or withholding of medication or treatment; intentional deprivation of sleep; imposition of fines (other than as reparation); and intimate physical searches of the child. Similar regulations under the Children Act come into effect in October 1991, and also cover private children's homes, which will be obliged to register with local authorities.

In Scotland, regulations applying to most categories of residential establishment providing accommodation for children prohibit corporal punishment, but do not cover other sanctions.

In England and Wales, regulations under the Children Act to be implemented in October 1991 will prevent local authority foster carers from using physical punishment on foster children (leaving children in care who are placed with their parents the only ones in care not protected against physical punishment and thus discriminated against over this issue). Guidance from the Department of

Health on children in group day care settings, nurseries, playgroups, childminding and out-of-school care also outlaws physical punishment.

But despite this progress, there is still not comprehensive and consistent protection for children against 'all forms of physical or mental violence'. There are no specific legal restrictions on sanctions in health institutions – either NHS or private. And some carers, in addition to parents and other relatives, appear to retain rights to smack – nannies, babysitters and private (not local authority) foster-parents (this last group could be forbidden from using physical punishment under Children Act regulations not yet (June 1991) published in draft).

It would be no more than logical (and in line with this article) to build on the progress there has been and make an explicit statement that children must be protected from physical punishment and other degrading or humiliating treatment when in the care of parents or anyone else. The experience of other countries indicates that such a move would also help prevent more serious abuse of children.

Protecting children without families

Article 20

'1. A child temporarily or permanently deprived of his or her family environment, or in whose own best interests cannot be allowed to remain in that environment, shall be entitled to special protection and assistance provided by the State.
2. States Parties shall in accordance with their national laws ensure alternative care for such a child.
3. Such care should include, *inter alia*, foster placement, Kafala of Islamic law, adoption, or if necessary placement in suitable institutions for the care of children. When considering solutions, due regard should be paid to the desirability of continuity in a child's upbringing and to the child's ethnic, religious, cultural and linguistic background.'

Local authority care is available under certain conditions for children and young people separated from parents. According to the first two paragraphs of this article, children and young people should receive 'special' protection and assistance, and if placed in institutions, these should be 'suitable'. Research on standards of care and education for children being looked after by local authorities, and individual cases exposing maltreatment of children in care, indicate that too frequently safeguards have been inadequate. The Children Act 1989, due to be implemented in October 1991, revises and improves the law on state care for children in England and Wales; existing law in Scotland and Northern Ireland is currently (June 1991) under review.

Assessment of children being looked after by local authorities before placement still frequently takes place in residential institutions such as 'observation and assessment centres': it is hard to see how such residential assessments (also common in health institutions) can provide useful or reliable information about the child's response to other environments.

The new emphasis on community care is also leading to a move away from institutional care. But some children and young people who are described as mentally ill, or who have disabilities or learning difficulties, may still spend significant periods of their lives in extremely unsuitable institutions, such as long-stay mental hospitals, or adult wards in psychiatric institutions. This article, read in conjunction with Article 2, should be implemented without discrimination on grounds of disability. While the number of children living full-time in long-stay mental hospitals is now very small, given the growing commitment to community care, there are still many single respite care placements of children in long-stay hospitals. Unless local authorities are resourced and positively directed to provide appropriate respite care arrangements for children as necessary in the community, inappropriate placements will continue. As the long-stay hospitals close, children may be placed in paediatric wards.

Relevant to the obligations of Article 20(3) is the new duty local authorities in England and Wales have under the Children Act (S. 22(5))to pay 'due consideration' to a child's 'religious persuasion, racial origin and cultural and linguistic background' when making decisions. Such duties should apply to health and education authorities, and to the proprietors of all private institutions looking after children (the Children Act does place a similar duty on voluntary organisations and proprietors of private – registered – children's homes looking after children). There is a further obligation (under Schedule 2, para. 12 of the Act) on local authorities to 'have regard to the different racial groups to which children within their area who are in need belong', when seeking to recruit foster carers. Collection of ethnic data, monitoring and evaluation are needed to ensure that in local authority assessment and placement policies and practice, no racial group is being treated less favourably in the provision of substitute care.

For children whose first language is not English, it is crucial that necessary help with learning their family language should be available at an early age; otherwise the opportunity is likely to be lost.

There are also new duties in the Children Act for local authorities in England and Wales looking after children to provide services 'to minimise the effect on disabled children ... of their disability' and 'to give such children the opportunity to lead lives which are as normal as possible' (Children Act 1989, Schedule 2, para. 6).

'Continuity' of placement is frequently not achieved for children in care, who may move through a succession of foster placements and institutional placements. The obligation of this article to provide continuity presents a challenge to authorities, demanding monitoring and a review of practice to ensure that there is maximum continuity for all children without discrimination – for example, currently children with disabilities and learning difficulties may suffer a disproportionate number of changes in placement (see also Article 23, page 85). All authorities should review current practice in the light of this article.

Adoption

Article 21

'States Parties which recognise and/or permit the system of adoption shall ensure that the best interests of the child shall be the paramount consideration and they shall:

(a) ensure that the adoption of a child is authorized only by competent authorities who determine, in accordance with applicable law and procedures and on the basis of all pertinent and reliable information, that the adoption is permissible in view of the child's status concerning parents, relatives and legal guardians and that, if required, the persons concerned have given their informed consent to the adoption on the basis of such counselling as may be necessary;

(b) recognise that intercountry adoption may be considered as an alternative means of child's care, if the child cannot be placed in a foster or an adoptive family or cannot in any suitable manner be cared for in the child's country of origin;

(c) ensure that the child concerned by intercountry adoption enjoys safeguards and standards equivalent to those existing in the case of national adoption;

(d) take all appropriate measures to ensure that, in intercountry adoption, the placement does not result in improper financial gain for those involved in it;

(e) promote, where appropriate, the objectives of this article by concluding bilateral or multilateral arrangements or agreements, and endeavour, within this framework, to ensure that the placement of the child in another country is carried out by competent authorities or organs.'

The 'best interests' of the child are the first consideration in adoption proceedings in the UK, but in the view of British Agencies for Adoption and Fostering (BAAF), current procedures do not satisfy Article 21(a): investigations are not necessarily adequate; counselling, if available at all, often takes place after the adoption. The current (1991) interdepartmental review of adoption law in England and Wales provides an opportunity for reform, using principles in the Convention as a basis.[63] (See also Articles 7 and 8, pages 23 and 28 children's rights to know and have contact with their parents).

The article refers to the informed consent of 'persons concerned': in England and Wales there is no provision for seeking the consent of children, although their views must be ascertained and taken into account. In Scotland, 'minor' children (girls from 12, boys from 14) have a right to consent or veto an adoption. When the Scottish Law Commission consulted recently on laws relating to minors and pupils, it suggested that the right to consent should be fixed at 16. But some respondents to the Commission's consultation disagreed, and the Commission was persuaded to change its recommendation, to propose that all children from the age of 12 should be able to consent or veto an adoption: 'Becoming a member, legally, of a new family is such an important step that it should not be imposed against the will of a child old enough to have a decided view'.[64]

Intercountry adoption raises serious children's rights issues. If the fundamental provisions of the Convention with regard to adequate health care for mothers and children (Article 24) and an adequate standard of living (Article 27) were fulfilled in all countries, it is unlikely that there would be any justification for frequent intercountry adoptions of babies or young children. The priority in resource-rich countries such as the UK, as reflected in Article 21(b), should be on contributing appropriately to aid programmes to diminish the justification for such adoptions. But at the moment it is clear that in individual cases, an intercountry adoption may be in the interests of a child who 'cannot in any suitable manner be cared for in the child's country of origin'.

In relation to Article 21(c), current safeguards are inadequate. The procedure is generally different, often with little official intervention, no formal 'approval' of adopters, and certainly no guarantee that the adoption is in the best interests of the child, or that in line with paragraphs (a) and (b), informed consent has been obtained, and there is no suitable way of caring for the child in his or her country of origin. Prospective adopters of children from overseas should be fully assessed and approved; there should be full preparation for transracial, transcultural adoptions, to ensure as far as possible no discrimination against such children in relation to other adopted children. Article 21(c) makes clear that standards and procedures for intercountry adoption should be equivalent to those for national adoptions.

On the issue of consent, a recent judgment made clear that English courts would demand proper evidence of consent for adoptions made overseas. The judgement concerned the adoption by an English couple of a four-week-old baby in China. When they returned to England they applied for an adoption order because English law would not recognise the Chinese adoption. They submitted that the Chinese order had the effect of extinguishing the relationship between biological mother and child, and so no consent was needed (and in any event the mother had consented to the making of the order in China). But the court did not accept this and said that enquiries would have to be made to establish the mother's current wishes.[65]

Children who are adopted overseas by British subjects may face discrimination because not all overseas adoptions are recognised under the Adoption (Designation of Overseas Adoptions) Order 1973 (although others may be recognised by courts). There should be clear criteria for this recognition, deriving from the best interests of the child. Currently children adopted outside the UK by British citizen parents may fail to gain British citizenship (see Article 7, page 23 and Article 10, page 36).

Children who have relatives in the UK who wish to bring them here for adoption often face long delays: such delays are only justified where they are due to thorough investigation of the child's current circumstances and family. It appears at present that such delays invariably involve children from New Commonwealth countries – suggesting discrimination in breach of Article 2.

Article 21(d) insists that there should be no improper financial gain for those involved in intercountry adoption: the current procedures do not guarantee this, and there have been allegations of what amounts to a trade in babies from certain countries. A lawyer in Colombia wrote to the Law Society in 1987, seeking adoption 'contracts', and suggesting that couples 'could join a good pleasure trip with an amazing and humane touch, having an adoption'. The Government must ensure that all intercountry adoptions are the responsibility of governmental or approved voluntary bodies, operating not for profit.

A start was made in 1990 on drawing up a new international convention on intercountry adoption, at a meeting convened by the Hague Conference on Private International Law. It was agreed that the starting point should be the relevant provisions in the UN

Convention, and that the essential aim was to combat trafficking, sale and other illicit or irresponsible acts; there should be effective 'central authorities' in both sending and receiving countries, responsible for supervising and monitoring intercountry adoptions and liaising with each other. The next meeting in 1991 will have before it an outline of the future convention and draft provisions; it is hoped a final draft will be prepared by 1993. The UK, in line with this article, should play a full part in promoting the principles underlying it in the international discussions.

Refugee children

Article 22

'1. States Parties shall take appropriate measures to ensure that a child who is seeking refugee status or who is considered a refugee in accordance with applicable international or domestic law and procedures shall, whether unaccompanied or accompanied by his or her parents or by any other person, receive appropriate protection and humanitarian assistance in the enjoyment of applicable rights set forth in this Convention and in other international human rights or humanitarian instruments to which the said States are Parties.

2. For this purpose, States Parties shall provide, as they consider appropriate, cooperation in any efforts by the United Nations and other competent intergovernmental organisations or non-government organizations cooperating with the United Nations to protect and assist such a child and to trace the parents or other members of the family of any refugee child in order to obtain information necessary for reunification with his or her family. In cases where no parents or other members of the family can be found, the child shall be accorded the same protection as any other child permanently or temporarily deprived of his or her family environment for any reason, as set forth in the present Convention.'

This article provides principles against which to test the UK's treatment of refugee children, and those seeking refugee status. The Refugee Council and other bodies involved in supporting refugee children and their families do not believe the implications of the article are yet accepted. There are obligations under Article 10 (see page 36) to deal with applications from a child or parents to enter the UK for the purpose of family reunification in a 'positive, humane and expeditious manner'. Most unaccompanied refugee children who are allowed to enter the UK are granted 'exceptional leave to remain' rather than refugee status, thus gaining no rights to family reunion here. The Refugee Council reports delays of up to four years in allowing immediate family to join children, in those cases in which applications are accepted.

The treatment of unaccompanied refugee children gives rise to serious concern. They have basic needs and rights as children, guaranteed under the various articles of the Convention, but in addition they lack the support of family or friends, and their language, culture and ethnicity may give rise to special needs. A report on the current situation by the Refugee Council (December 1990) noted that the Council had been aware of 40 to 50 children arriving in the UK unaccompanied each year. In August and September 1990 at least 170 unaccompanied children arrived from Eritrea: 'This has focused attention on the appalling lack of resources which exist for such refugee children'. The report indicates that at least 25 children were held in detention by the Immigration Service on arrival; 70 children had to wait for up to three months before a local authority responded to their needs; at least 50 children were moved more than three times during their first three months in the UK; at least 130 children did not speak English, and at least 50, following local authority placement, had no access to support from people of their own culture and language. The report also indicates that some children are not identified at ports of entry, and have not emerged as being in need of care or support:

> 'They are either surviving on their own or being cared for by someone, somewhere. This group might cover children from a wide range of countries and age groups. Without proper co-ordination and improved services, such children are extraordinarily vulnerable to exploitation, abuse and oppression.'[67]

There is currently no clear responsibility for the reception and short-term care of unaccompanied refugee children (it appears that on occasion even young children are placed initially in immigration detention centres or even police cells) nor for their assessment or longer-term placement and support. The United Nations High Commissioner for Refugees has expressed concern to ministers about this issue. At central government level, the Home Office, Foreign Office, and Departments of Health, Education and Science, and Environment appear to share some responsibility for these children. The Refugee Council's Working Group on Unaccompanied Refugee Children and Adolescents has proposed a recognised central agency to coordinate and develop care arrangements for newly identified unaccompanied children.[67] The same agency could run specialist reception facilities, able to assess individual children's needs adequately, as well as develop suitable longer term arrangements on behalf of local authorities.

The last sentence of Article 22(2) emphasises that standards of care for such unaccompanied children should be the same as for any other children in the UK temporarily deprived of their family environment. The Children Act (S.17)places obligations on local authorities in England and Wales towards 'children in need' in their area; it is to be hoped that authorities – in particular those near to ports of entry – will receive specific guidance on support and care for unaccompanied refugee children. A letter to directors of social services in England and Wales from the Chief Inspector of the Social Services Inspectorate, sent out in January 1991, indicated that responsibility for the child lies with the local authority in which the child is physically present when his or her unaccompanied situation comes to the attention of social services. The particular case of unaccompanied refugee children is not to be covered in guidance issued under the Children Act, but 'practice guidance' for local authorities may be issued.

Currently guidelines from the United Nations High Commissioner for Refugees are not fully implemented in the UK; these guidelines suggest, for example, that determination of the status of refugee or asylum-seeking children should involve childcare experts, same-language speakers and the appointment of a 'guardian'.[68]

Children with disabilities and learning difficulties

Article 23

'1. States Parties recognize that a mentally or physically disabled child should enjoy a full and decent life, in conditions which ensure dignity, promote self-reliance, and facilitate the child's active participation in the community.

2. States Parties recognize the right of the disabled child to special care and shall encourage and ensure the extension, subject to available resources, to the eligible child and those responsible for his or her care, of assistance for which application is made and which is appropriate to the child's condition and to the circumstances of the parents or others caring for the child.

3. Recognizing the special needs of a disabled child, assistance extended in accordance with paragraph 2 shall be provided free of charge, whenever possible, taking into account the financial resources of the parents or others caring for the child, and shall be designed to ensure that the disabled child has effective access to and receives education, training, health care services, rehabilitation services, preparation for employment and recreation opportunities in a manner conducive to the child's achieving the fullest possible social integration and individual development, including his or her cultural and spiritual development.

4. States Parties shall promote in the spirit of international co-operation the exchange of appropriate information in the field of preventive health care and of medical, psychological and functional treatment of disabled children, including dissemination of and access to information concerning methods of rehabilitation, education and vocational services, with the aim of enabling States Parties to improve their capabilities and skills and to widen their experience in these areas. In this regard, particular account shall be taken of the needs of developing countries.'

Article 2 of the Convention guarantees all the rights safeguarded by it without discrimination on grounds of disability. Article 23 sets out special rights for children with disabilities and learning difficulties. Placement of children with disabilities and learning difficulties in long-term residential settings – hospitals, mental nursing homes, residential care homes, independent boarding schools, residential non-maintained special schools, and so on – is not compatible with the requirement for a 'full and decent life ensuring the child's active participation in the community'. The Children Act 1989 and the National Health Service and Community Care Act 1990 could, if implemented with adequate resources (and without imposing new and discriminatory charges on carers), improve the lives of many children. The Children Act contains an important new duty for local authority social services departments in England and Wales to provide services 'designed (a) to minimise the effect on disabled children within their area of their disabilities; and (b) to give such children the opportunity to lead lives which are as normal as possible'.

Dangers of individual children being 'lost' and forgotten in obscure residential placements, out of touch with their families and with inadequate assessment and monitoring, should reduce with new duties in the Children Act: health and education authorities must notify the appropriate social services department if they are accommodating a child for more than three months, and the social services department must satisfy itself that the child's welfare is being adequately safeguarded and promoted. Authorities must also take steps to help children they are not looking after but who are living away from home, to enable them to live at home, or to 'promote contact' between children and their families.

A recent report from the Office of Population Censuses and Surveys showed that 49 per cent of children with disabilities living in local authority homes received no parental visits at all, compared with 42 per cent of all children living in communal residential institutions; 58 per cent of children in local authority homes never went out to visit parents, compared with 53 per cent overall.[69] The report also showed that 45 per cent of all children with disabilities in residential institutions had not been on a special group holiday during the previous year (and for most of those who had a holiday, it only lasted a week). Other reports in the same series highlight the effect on parents or carers and other children of having a child with a disability living at home, given inadequate levels of support and continuing prejudice.

The movement of children out of long-term mental hospital places is almost completed – a few teenagers sadly remain who will move into adult accommodation in the next year or two. But many children are readmitted for frequent respite care periods (10,000 to 11,000 admissions in a recent year; the monitoring does not reveal how many individual children are involved in these placements) and children are still being placed in inappropriate adult wards. It is unclear what will happen when the final children's wards or units are closed. Evidence from the Family Fund and other sources suggests that there are more children with complex and multiple disabilities not easily met in local authority provision as organised at present. The growing use of private residential homes and independent boarding schools as a stopgap measure gives rise to further concern.

There has been an encouraging growth in adoption and long-term fostering arrangements, with specialist agencies like Parents for Children demonstrating that it is possible to find and sustain family placements for children with complex disabilities.

But 'facilitating active participation in the community' and 'achieving the fullest possible social integration' are targets far from being achieved for many children who come within the scope of this article. Education in an ordinary school with children without disabilities and learning difficulties is still not seen as a right, alongside other equal opportunities principles. The Education Act 1981 and similar legislation for Scotland (see also Articles 28 and 29, pages 109 and 114) provide very limited obligations to stop segregation of children with special educational needs in special schools, limiting the principle by various conditions including 'efficient use of resources'. The Act does, however, provide a positive duty to ensure proper integration of children with special educational needs once in ordinary schools. (The inclusion of the phrase 'subject to available resources' in paragraph 2 of this particular article in itself seems discriminatory. Article 4 emphasises that overall obligations to implement economic, social and cultural rights in the Convention are limited to 'the maximum extent of (the State's) available resources'.)

There is widespread concern among local education authorities (LEAs) about resources for meeting pupils' special educational needs in mainstream schools. A survey conducted by the Special Needs Advisory Council in April 1990 found that of the 48 per cent of LEAs which responded, 64 per cent reported that changes in funding arrangements and shortfalls in local allocation of resources meant they would experience problems in the future. Several LEAs state that they should not be compelled under the new arrangements for Local Management of Schools (LMS) to delegate important support services for special educational needs which they believe can be operated more efficiently from the centre.

Only systematic monitoring can reveal how such changes as LMS, and the National Curriculum, affect children with disabilities and learning difficulties. The obligations under this article, and to provide a right to education based on equal opportunities under Article 28, should provide a spur for national and local policy reviews. Monitoring of special education policy and practice must include collection of ethnic data; the limited research there has been suggests a disproportionate number of children from certain ethnic groups in certain categories of special school.[70]

Segregated schooling

While local education authorities continue to maintain a variety of segregated special schools, they can argue that it is not an 'efficient use of resources' to develop properly supported integration in ordinary schools and colleges. According to a report published in February 1991 by the Centre for Studies on Integration in Education, 15 LEAs significantly increased the proportion of children they sent to separate special schools between 1982 and 1990; three of them (Doncaster, Rotherham and St Helens) by more than a quarter.[71] The proportion of children aged five and over segregated in special schools in England fell overall only slightly from 1.72 per cent in 1982 to 1.59 per cent in January 1990. There are also vast regional differences in policy and practice: in Cornwall in 1990, 0.62 per cent of the authority's school population was in segregated special schools, as against 3.98 per cent in the London Borough of Lambeth and 3.43 per cent in the London Borough of Hackney. Twenty-two LEAs have more than 2 per cent of their school population in separate special schools. Only five of the 108 LEAs in England and Wales have less than 1 per cent. Fifteen LEAs did cut their levels of segregation between 1982 and 1990 by 25 per cent or more (Bradford, Leeds and Richmond in Surrey by more than 40 per cent).

The report also reveals that 12 per cent of the special school population in Engalnd are in independent special schools (11,812 in January 1990). Again, there are wide variations between authorities: a child in the London Borough of Ealing is 30 times more likely than a child in Leeds to be sent to an independent special school.

There is clearly wide discrimination by region in children's rights to placement in mainstream education.

The appeals process to challenge placement decisions for children who get statements of special needs under the Education Act 1981 in England and Wales discriminates against these children and their parents: appeal committees hearing appeals on 'ordinary' school choice under the Education Act 1980 can overturn LEA decisions; those hearing 1981 Act appeals can only refer back decisions for reconsideration. In addition, and in breach of Article 12 of the Convention (see page 44), children themselves have no say in or right to challenge these decisions, only parents. In Scotland, the appeals process relating to special needs has the same powers as for ordinary school choice appeals.

With reference to Article 23(3), there is widespread concern that the statementing process under the 1981 Act is not achieving its aim of ensuring that special educational needs are met in England and Wales: professionals assessing children have complained that their recommendations following assessment are 'censored' by LEAs, because the latter do not wish to be committed to provision they do not have the resources to provide. It also appears that there are still a large number of children with special educational needs in special schools in some LEAs who do not have the protection of a statement (DES statistics for 1986 showed seven LEAs in which over 80 per cent of these children were still without a statement three years after full implementation of the 1981 Act).

Transition to adult services poses a special problem for many children with disabilities and learning difficulties. The obligation to maintain a statement for those children and young people who have one ends when they leave school. There is no obligation to maintain statements, with the corresponding legal safeguards, for young people who move into further education at 16. This is discriminatory. Full implementation of the Disabled Persons (Services, Consultation and Representation) Act 1986 would make a positive contribution, but no date has been set.

Health and health services

Article 24

'1. States Parties recognize the right of the child to the enjoyment of the highest attainable standard of health and to facilities for the treatment of illness and rehabilitation of health. States Parties shall strive to ensure that no child is deprived of his or her right of access to such health care services.

2. States Parties shall pursue full implementation of this right and, in particular, shall take appropriate measures:

(a) to diminish infant and child mortality,

(b) to ensure the provision of necessary medical assistance and health care to all children with emphasis on the development of primary health care,

(c) to combat disease and malnutrition including within the framework of primary health care, through *inter alia* the application of readily available technology and through the provision of adequate nutritious foods and clean drinking water, taking into consideration the dangers and risks of environmental pollution,

(d) to ensure appropriate pre- and post-natal health care for mothers,

(e) to ensure that all segments of society, in particular parents and children, are informed, have access to education and are supported in the use of, basic knowledge of child health and nutrition, the advantages of breast-feeding, hygiene and environmental sanitation and the prevention of accidents,

(f) to develop preventive health care, guidance for parents, and family planning education and services.

3. States Parties shall take all effective and appropriate measures with a view to abolishing traditional practices prejudicial to the health of children.

4. States Parties undertake to promote and encourage international co-operation with a view to achieving progressively the full realization of the right recognized in this article. In this regard, particular account shall be taken of the needs of developing countries.'

Article 24(1)

Full implementation of this article implies setting standards for children's health services, and having agreed national policies to diminish inequalities to the maximum extent possible. The formula for allocating resources within the National Health Service does not, in the view of the British Paediatric Association and others, reflect the needs of children. Article 24, taken in conjunction with Article 2, implies not discriminating in the provision of 'the highest attainable standard of health' and health facilities. Regional variations in health care are well documented, as are variations in, for example, infant mortality rates by social class and ethnic background (see Article 6, page 19).

The National Study of Health and Growth has surveyed children aged from four to 11 since 1972 in England and Scotland: the surveys indicated trends towards taller children from 1972 to 1979, but between 1979 and 1986 this slowed or stopped altogether.[72] A 1989 survey, *Diets of British Schoolchildren* found evidence that children from families in which the father is unemployed, or from families receiving benefits, are significantly shorter; children from 'higher' social classes are taller than others.[73]

Article 24(2)

The sub-paragraphs of Article 24(2) are considered individually below:

Article 24(2)(a)

There has been a continuing fall in the infant mortality rate (with a very small upward 'hiccup' in this downward trend in 1986). There is a detailed discussion of the rates and their variation by social class, region, and so on, as well as comparisons with other countries, in *Child Poverty and Deprivation in the UK*.[74] The decline in the infant mortality rate in the 1980s was much slower than in the previous decade. While it is arguable that infant mortality becomes harder to reduce below a certain level, rates in the UK have declined very much more slowly than in some other countries and (at 8.4 per thousand live births in 1989) are still high in comparison with, for example, France (7.9 in 1986); Italy (8.1 in 1985) and Sweden (5.9 in 1986). If the UK rate had matched that of Sweden in 1986, 2,247 children in England and Wales would not have died. The UK had the highest post-neonatal mortality rate (children dying between the ages of five weeks and one year, per 1,000 live births) of seven Western countries recorded in a study published in 1990. The only group recording a higher rate was that of US Blacks.[75]

There are sharp variations in infant death by social class, by region and by country of birth of mother (see Article 6, page 19).

Article 24(2)(b)

It is too early to judge the full effects of changes in the administration and delivery of the National Health Service on children, but commentators fear that the proportion of resources spent on children may decline, and may be even less equitably distributed across the UK; services for children may become more fragmented; new incentives for GP budget-holders may operate to the disadvantage of their child patients; and socio-economic differences in access to health services for children may be increased (for a fuller discussion see *Working for Children? Children's Services and the NHS Review*.[76] A survey in 1983 found that some health districts ran five times more health clinics than others, with no obvious relation between provision and need.[77] Close and detailed monitoring is required to reveal whether this provision of the Convention is fully implemented in the UK.

Article 24(2)(c)

Immunisation rates still give cause for concern in the UK, with wide variations between regions, and lower overall rates than in many other countries, but there have been recent improvements in overall rates. In 1985 the Government accepted the World Health Organisation target of 90 per cent immunisation by 1990, as a step towards eliminating certain diseases by 2000. According to the Department of Health, in November 1990 the national average immunisation rate for diphtheria, tetanus and polio was 90 per cent, for measles, mumps and rubella 88 per cent, and for whooping cough 83 per cent. Nineteen district health authorities (DHAs) had reached the 90 per cent target for all seven immunisable diseases, 96 per cent for measles, mumps and rubella. The Department suggests that indigenous diphtheria, neonatal tetanus and poliomyelitis have all been effectively eliminated.[78]

There is concern that standards of nutrition for children have declined during the 1980s, because of the abolition of price maintenance and the nutritional standards for school meals. Three-quarters of children are estimated to have excessive fat intake. Scottish primary schoolchildren have been found to be low on vitamin C and beta carotene. Older children, particularly girls, taking food out of school have the poorest diets. Where school meals are taken, they contain between 30 and 43 per cent of the average daily energy intake. Several studies of families receiving benefit have found gross inadequacies in diet, with serious deficiencies of minerals and vitamin C.[79]

Nutrition and diet may be a particular issue for children from minority ethnic groups in institutions: care needs to be taken to ensure that arrangements sensitive to their needs are made.

The Water Act 1990 sets out a statutory framework for drinking water quality, incorporating standards set by European Community Directive 80/778/EEC. The Directive was issued in 1980 for compliance by 1985. But several of its requirements are still frequently breached by much British tapwater. In 1989 an action was brought against the UK Government before the Court of Justice of the European Communities, by the Commission of the EC, protesting against lack of compliance with the Directive, in particular over high nitrate levels (29 supply zones not complying with the maximum admissible concentration); lead levels (according to the Commission's information the problem extends throughout Scotland); and the absence of binding provisions implementing the Directive in full (the regulations under the Water Act do not apply to Scotland and Northern Ireland, and do not apply to water used in the food production industry). The case continues.[80] The effects of water pollution, and other forms of environmental pollution, are particularly serious for pregnant women and for babies and children.

Many of our beaches also remain heavily polluted, in breach of EC standards (Bathing Waters Directive 76/160/EEC, which should have been fully implemented by 1985) and pose a particular health hazard for children. In 1987, 163 of the 360 identified bathing waters around the UK did not meet EC standards. In 1990 an action was brought against the UK at the Court of Justice for non-compliance, mentioning in particular the quality of bathing waters in Blackpool, and adjacent to Southport and Formby.[81] The case continues.

Air pollution remains a serious problem: European Community Directive 80/779/EEC was issued in 1980 for implementation by 1982. But recently there were still 22 UK cities, mainly in the north of England and Belfast in Northern Ireland, which did not comply.

The Government is committed to full compliance by 1993. In 1974, a paper from the Medical Research Council's Air Pollution Unit presented to a paediatric conference stated: 'There is by now evidence of an association between the general prevalence of respiratory illnesses in children and the amounts of pollution in the areas where they live'.[82]

Passive smoking is increasingly recognised as a serious form of air pollution threatening to health – particularly children's health: an Australian Court recently confirmed after reviewing scientific evidence that passive smoking caused respiratory diseases in young children, asthma and lung cancer. The case was brought by the Australian Federation of Consumer Organisations against the Tobacco Institute of Australia, over misleading advertisements which claimed 'There is little evidence and nothing which proves scientifically that cigarette smoke causes diseases in non-smokers'. The judge banned the advertisement under the Trade Practices Act, stating:

> 'Active smokers are likely to be misled by the statement into believing their smoking does not prejudice the health of non-smokers, particularly small children. Non-smokers are likely to be deceived or misled into believing cigarette smoke does not affect their own health or the health of their children. These are serious matters.'[83]

Damp conditions in housing also threaten children's health. A recent large-scale study reported in the *British Medical Journal* found:

> 'Children living in damp and mouldy dwellings had a greater prevalence of respiratory symptoms (wheeze, sore throat, runny nose) and headaches and fever compared with those living in dry dwellings . . . All these differences persisted after controlling for possible confounding factors such as household income, cigarette smoking, unemployment and overcrowding. Damp and mouldy living conditions have an adverse effect on symptomatic health, particularly among children.'

It comments that poor housing conditions are an important public health issue, not solely for their immediate impact, but also for long-term implications: 'Poor housing conditions in childhood for example are associated with higher rates of admission to hospital and higher morbidity and mortality in adult life'.[84]

Instances of childhood leukaemia in the vicinity of nuclear installations have led to much concern and investigation. Most recently, a study in West Cumbria (the area of the Sellafield nuclear plant) suggested that the risk to children was raised if they had a father employed in the plant, particularly if the father had had relatively high exposure to radiation before the affected children were conceived.[85] The report of the study concluded that until the findings from other studies are available, 'workers need to be counselled and those who have not yet completed their families should be advised to avoid high exposures'.

Article 24(2)(d)

There are serious regional variations in ante- and post-natal care. High rates of attendance for ante-natal care are agreed to be related to low rates of mortality and morbidity. Attempts to reduce class variations in attendance have been very successful in some areas of the UK: consistent national targets are required.

Article 24(2)(e)

Health education has undoubtedly developed over recent decades, but there is no statutory duty to provide it for either children or adults. By the early 1980s school inspectors found that roughly 68 per cent of secondary schools and 30 per cent of primary schools had a planned programme of health education; between a third and a half of secondary schools had a coordinator to plan health education across the curriculum. In 1981, the Department of Education recognised that health education should be an important part of the curriculum for every pupil, but the legislation imposing a National Curriculum, implemented in England and Wales under the Education Reform Act 1988, makes no provision for it.

While the advantages of breast-feeding are recognised and promoted by the Government through the Health Education Authority, little has been done to provide facilities for breast-feeding mothers in public and other buildings, and to encourage public acceptance of it. Comparative figures in UNICEF's report *The State of the World's Children 1991* suggest that Britain has a very low proportion of mothers breast-feeding – 26 per cent at three months, and 22 per cent at six months.[86]

Prevention of accidents to children in the UK is another cause for concern: accidents are now the single largest cause of death for children and young adults, with motor accidents accounting for the majority of accidental deaths after age four. In 1988, 360 children aged under 14 died in transport-related accidents, and 171 died in home accidents – 100 from burns.[87]

Accidents are more common among lower socio-economic groups, for example, boys in lower social classes are eight times more likely to be killed in motor-related accidents than those from higher social classes.[88]

The UK has a comparatively long way to go to reduce its child accident rate to that of other European countries, in particular the Scandinavian countries.

Article 24(2)(f)

While there is clearly increasing emphasis placed on preventive health care in the NHS and in health education, there is concern at variations in its effectiveness. Potential limitations on provision of sex education in school contained in recent education legislation (see Article 13, page 50) may threaten some young people's access to information about family planning services.

Article 24(3)

Article 24(3) raises some sensitive cultural and religious issues. There is legislation in the UK against female circumcision, the Prohibition of Female Circumcision Act 1985. But it is not effective in ending the practice, and there have been very few prosecutions under it. A recent BBC television documentary indicated that many Black British primary schoolgirls are still suffering illegal genital mutilation. A GP working in Tower Hamlets in London wrote about the documentary in the *British Medical Journal*: 'As a GP ... I come across circumcised Somali women. The BBC film ... showed how important it is that doctors do not remain silent but speak out against this ritual'.[89]

Male circumcision is a declining but still widespread practice. In the mid-1980s, 76 per cent of boys born in America still had the operation. Since the early 1970s medical authorities on both sides of the Atlantic have declared that 'there are no medical indications for routine circumcision of the newborn'. Research findings which suggested that male circumcision might reduce the incidence of cancer of the cervix in female partners have been discounted, and it has been shown that the protection which it offers from (very rare) cancer of the penis is no greater than that afforded by reasonable personal hygiene. Circumcision nevertheless continues for nonmedical reasons.[90] As well as families for whom the practice is part of religious ritual, some suggest that the practice is part of a child's cultural identity on the basis of 'like father, like son'. Nevertheless, circumcision is normally carried out long before the child can give an informed consent, and is an invasion of the child's physical integrity. Circumcision is sometimes carried out by adults with no formal medical training. There is evidence that the practice can lead to infection, injury and mutilation for a significant number of children. In her classic book on child development, first published in 1974, Penelope Leach quotes a national study of 2,428 children of whom 24 per cent had been circumcised. At that date she noted that the Registrar General's returns showed around 16 deaths every year as a result of complications from circumcision, and that around 22 per cent of baby boys suffered some complication from the operation – usually haemorrhage or sepsis. 'If the operation is to be carried out, even on a newborn, parents should not allow themselves to be persuaded that the infant is not old enough to feel pain. Circumcision without anaesthetic is cruel'.[91] The most recent estimate of serious infections is two or three per cent. Among these are skin infections, bloodstream infections, bleeding, gangrene, scarring and various surgical accidents', according to the American medical commentator quoted above. Although anaesthesia is now more widely recommended, the procedure is still often carried out with none.

Other practices, including piercing of ears and/or nose without the informed consent of children, are also unjustified, even if traditional, practices which may be prejudicial to health. In any case they invade the physical integrity of the child. The practice of physical punishment of children (barred by Article 19, see page 71) could be described as a common 'traditional practice' in the UK which is detrimental to the health – both physical and psychological – of children.

Article 24(4)

While worldwide more than a quarter of a million small children are dying every week of easily preventable disease and malnutrition, our own targets to create adequate health services for children in the UK may seem a less urgent priority. Article 24(4) emphasises the obligation of all countries to cooperate, in particular to help develop rights to health for children in developing countries. The British Overseas Aid 1990 Annual Review emphasises that the Overseas

Development Agency's priority in the sector of health and population is currently to 'help bring affordable and appropriate health-care services to the poorest sections of the community, particularly mothers and children'.[92] (see also Article 4, page 15)

Periodic review of placement and treatment of children

Article 25

'States Parties recognize the right of a child who has been placed by the competent authorities for the purposes of care, protection, or treatment of his or her physical or mental health, to a periodic review of the treatment provided to the child and all other circumstances relevant to his or her placement.'

For the first time, detailed regulations are to be issued under the Children Act 1989 on the duties of social services departments in England and Wales to review children they are looking after. The Act ensures that the authority seeks the child's own views before a review, and notifies the child of the results of the review. It is not yet clear whether children will have a right to be present at their reviews, although Article 12 of the Convention (see page 44) would suggest that they should have. Draft regulations issued by the Department of Health state that authorities should 'so far as is practicable' involve the child 'in the review, including where the authority consider appropriate the attendance [of the child] at part or all of any meeting'. Children placed in voluntary children's homes and private (registered) homes, even if not in care, will be covered by similar review duties relating to the voluntary organisation or person running the home (Children Act 1989, S. 26, 59, and schedule 6, para 10). The group currently reviewing childcare law in Scotland has proposed that children aged 12 and over should have a right to attend, and that requests to attend from younger children should be considered in the light of their age and capacity to understand; care authorities should be required to prepare children and young people for attendance.[93]

The placement of children in 'secure accommodation' (lock-ups in the childcare system) must be reviewed within one month (this is a new requirement in regulations issued under the Children Act 1989 for England and Wales) and then at intervals not exceeding three months (Children and Young Persons (Secure Accommodation) Regulations).

There are also new duties in the Act to ensure that health and education authorities in England and Wales who accommodate or plan to accommodate any child for more than three months inform the 'responsible local authority', which has a duty to ensure that the welfare of the child is adequately safeguarded and promoted, and to consider whether it should take other action. A similar duty to inform the authority is placed on the proprietors of certain institutions – residential care homes, nursing homes and mental nursing homes.

But these duties (which do not as yet apply in Scotland and Northern Ireland, where legislation is currently (June 1991) under review) do not in themselves imply a review of the same thoroughness as that proposed for children in care. There are no formal requirements to review the placement and treatment of children and young people who are admitted by their parents as informal patients in hospitals, including mental illness and mental handicap hospitals, adolescent units, and private health institutions, although official guidance promotes this. A study of all children detained in the UK, *Children in Custody*, published in 1987, suggested that there were up to 1,500 detained informal child patients in mental illness and mental handicap hospitals and units.[94] While the reporting duty under the Children Act referred to above should ensure that such children are no longer 'lost' in institutions, it will not necessarily lead to adequate reviews of their treatment. Detention of this kind also raises issues under Article 37 of the UN Convention (see page 134) and under Article 5 of the European Convention on Human Rights. Children aged under 16 who are detained under the Mental Health Act 1983 must have their placement reviewed by a Mental Health Review Tribunal within a year of admission or of the previous review.

Children and young people compulsorily assessed and placed under the Education Act 1981 and similar legislation in Scotland and Northern Ireland because of emotional and behavioural difficulties come within the scope of this article. The Act does place duties on local education authorities to review each year children with 'statements' ('records' in Scotland) of special educational needs annually. However, there are no detailed requirements about the scope of the review (and no obligation to involve the child).

Social security

Article 26

'1. States Parties shall recognize for every child the right to benefit from social security, including social insurance, and shall take the necessary measures to achieve the full realization of this right in accordance with their national law.

2. The benefits should, where appropriate, be granted taking into account the resources and the circumstances of the child and persons having responsibility for the maintenance of the child as well as any other consideration relevant to an application for benefits made by or on behalf of the child.'

Over the last decade there has been a very substantial increase in the number of children in families who are dependent on social security benefit, so the adequacy of such benefit is particularly crucial to children (see Jonathan Bradshaw's *Child Poverty and Deprivation in the UK*[95]). Commentators suggest that changes in social security over the 1980s have affected children more than adults, and generally for the worse. Higher percentages of children live in poverty than adults.[96] The level of universal child benefit in the UK (not generous by the standards of other European countries) was frozen for three years and is only being increased in 1991 for the first or eldest eligible child. Money is more likely to benefit children if it is clearly labelled as 'children's money', as child benefit is, and not just lost in, for example income support or tax allowances. It is also beneficial to children that child benefit is paid to the 'main carer'.

Means-tested benefits help children only in families where the total income is below a certain level. This does nothing for those children in families where total income is above the poverty line but not shared appropriately: the child's right to benefit from social security must be protected under this article. The means-tested benefit for low-wage families – family credit – is believed to be being claimed by just over half of those eligible which is relevant to implementation of the first paragraph of Article 26(1). And other means tested benefits tend to be disproportionately underclaimed by families with children.

Most young people aged 16 and 17 lost their entitlement to income support in September 1988. The assumption now is that young people of this age should either stay at school or college while living at home, or find a job, or find a place on a youth training scheme. The Government's intention is that there should be a youth training place for all young people leaving full-time education who have no job. In fact it appears that there are often delays before places, or appropriate places, are available, and a bridging allowance can only be claimed for eight weeks.

The only young people who retain a right to income support are those in categories who are not required to sign on as a condition of entitlement to benefit – for example, because of single parenthood, sickness or disability. In addition, certain young people can claim income support after leaving school for a period of up to 16 weeks, depending on when they leave. This period, known as the child benefit extension period, applies to young people in very limited categories: those with no living parents or guardian; those who have been in care and not living with parents prior to their sixteenth birthday; those who are living away from parents, either because of physical or sexual abuse, or because of disability, learning difficulty or mental illness; those who are living alone because parents are ill, in custody or unable to enter the UK; and those who are living in accommodation as part of a rehabilitation programme supervised by social services or the probation service. Once the extension period is exhausted, young people in these categories can only obtain benefit if they apply to the Secretary of State to exercise discretion and award benefit for a further limited period on the grounds that otherwise 'severe hardship' would occur. There is no right of appeal against the Secretary of State's decision.

Changes were also introduced, in April 1988, to the level of benefits paid to young people: age rather than circumstance determines the level of benefit. Three tiers were introduced: for those aged 16 and 17 £21.90 per week; those aged between 18 and 24 £28.80; and those aged 25 and over £36.70 (February 1991 rates). After representations, the Government introduced some changes in July 1989, so that those aged 16 and 17 who are forced to live independently can claim at the rate for 18 to 24-year-olds (though this rate is quite inadequate for independent living in any case). An additional category of young people who are genuinely estranged from their parents was added to those who can claim for a limited period on grounds of severe hardship; young people in night shelters are automatically considered for claims of severe hardship.

The National Association of Citizens Advice Bureaux (NACAB) asked local bureaux for information about social security enquiries received from young people. A report published in October 1989 emphasised that the 'concessions' made by the Government had had 'little impact on the number of young people facing poverty'.[97] NACAB identified two problems:

'First, the criteria for eligibility are still extremely tightly drawn and allow numbers of 16-17 year-olds to remain unprotected. Second, even where a young person clearly comes within the definition of severe hardship, they are often not informed that they are entitled to help.'

One bureau (Norwich) wrote:

'We had a large influx of clients with problems of this nature earlier in the year and it is still causing considerable concern ... We have seen a greater incidence of relationship breakdown and homelessness among young people in the Norwich area and have received reports of young people sleeping rough at bus stations and in the casualty ward of local hospitals. This practice has been common enough to force hospitals to fit locks on their doors in order to prevent access by homeless young people at night.'

NACAB comments:

'Young people feel helpless, resentful, humiliated and frustrated. Parents are often confused and angry when faced with the reality of a system which offers neither them nor the young person any means of support. This situation inevitably produces tension and conflict and can be destructive of family relationships.'

The NACAB report highlights the problems of pregnant women under 18, who are unable to claim income support until six months pregnant. Those over 18 unable to find work can claim throughout their pregnancy.

'The consequences of poor eating in early pregnancy can be detrimental and have permanent implications for the future health of the baby and can also seriously undermine the health of the mother. It is a matter therefore of profound concern that there are 16-17 year olds who are pregnant, lacking entitlement to benefit and who cannot obtain help from elsewhere.'

Implementation of the Convention in the UK should include a review of social security legislation based on the right of children in families to an adequate level of benefit, and of young people to receive an adequate level of benefit in their own right. Currently, the obligations of this article are not being fulfilled for many children and for young people aged 16 and 17, leading to a less than adequate standard of living (see Article 27 below). It is important to ensure that social security rights are fulfilled for all children and young people without discrimination, for example on grounds of disability (see Article 18, page 64, and Article 23, page 86, for further discussion of economic consequences of disability for children and families). It is also important to ensure that benefits are able to support arrangements for shared care of children.

Standard of living

Article 27

'1. States Parties recognize the right of every child to a standard of living adequate for the child's physical, mental, spiritual, moral and social development.

2. The parent(s) or others responsible for the child have the primary responsibility to secure, within their abilities and financial capacities, the conditions of living necessary for the child's development.

3. States Parties in accordance with national conditions and within their means shall take appropriate measures to assist parents and others responsible for the child to implement this right and shall in case of need provide material assistance and support programmes, particularly with regard to nutrition, clothing and housing.

4. States Parties shall take all appropriate measures to secure the recovery of maintenance for the child from the parents or other persons having financial responsibility for the child, both within the State Party and from abroad. In particular, where the person having financial responsibility for the child lives in a State different from that of the child, States Parties shall promote the accession to international agreements or the conclusion of such agreements as well as the making of other appropriate arrangements.'

There is sufficient evidence to suggest that this article is not adequately implemented for children in the UK. The UK contribution to a UNICEF comparative study of child poverty and deprivation in the industrialised countries, published at the end of 1990, found: 'Perhaps the most important conclusion to be drawn from this review is that there is a need to develop better mechanisms than we have for monitoring the state of children in the UK'. But the report also concluded:

'During the 1980s children have borne the brunt of the changes that have occurred in the economic conditions, demographic structure and social policies of the UK. More children have been living in low income families and the number of children living in poverty has doubled. Inequalities have also become wider. There is no evidence that improvements in the living standards of the better off have 'trickled down' to low income families with children.'

This study provides a comprehensive analysis of the available information on child poverty, its causes and effects.[98]

The lives of many thousands of children whose families are dependent on benefit are impoverished in many ways, and they are also most likely to be living in areas where services – health, education and social services – are hard-pressed. A study of a sample of two-parent families with children with an unemployed head living on supplementary benefit in the North-East of England in 1988 concluded:

> 'The picture which emerges from this detailed study of family lives is one of constant restriction in almost every aspect of people's activities ... The lives of these families, and perhaps most seriously the lives of the children in them, are marked by the unrelieved struggle to manage with dreary diets and drab clothing.
>
> They also suffer what amounts to cultural imprisonment in their homes in our society in which getting out with money to spend on recreation and leisure is normal at every other income level.'

Families commented on the restrictions on their children's lives: 'They are not being able to do the same things as their friends. They don't get any treats. They don't have many clothes.' ... 'The kids don't go out anywhere. They never get days out.' ... 'We get ratty with them. They don't get what they need.'[99]

In some areas of the country, the proportion of families and children living in poverty is particularly high: in Northern Ireland, in the period 1983-5, it is estimated that 39 per cent of children were living in poverty (below 50 per cent of average income).[100]

The second and third paragraphs of the article emphasise the primary responsibility of parents for their children's standard of living, and the State's obligation to assist them and provide 'material assistance and support programmes, particularly with regard to nutrition, clothing and housing'. Concern over nutrition of children was discussed in the context of Article 24 (see page 92).

There have been studies of unemployed families' and single parents' expenditure on their children's clothing, which have concluded that they are unable to maintain minimum necessary stocks of clothing.[101] A study comparing the clothing stocks of families with an unemployed head with minimum standards found that 60 per cent of children were below standard on two or more essential items.[102]

Homelessness has increased in the last decade, and many children are affected, although single people, including young people who have left home, are probably hardest hit. Seventy-nine per cent of homeless households in priority need in 1988 included dependent children and/or pregnant women.[103] A working party of the Association of Metropolitan Authorities found that 'black households are some three or four times as likely to become statutorily homeless as white households'.[104] The removal of entitlement to social security for young people aged 16 and 17, and reductions for older young people (see page 102) have increased homelessness among them. Large numbers of children are living in 'bed and breakfast' accommodation, raising concerns about health, development, safety, education and diet. Poor families with children are most likely to be living in public sector housing in urban areas. A recent survey of a random sample of 579 families with children in Glasgow, Edinburgh and London found that a third of dwellings contained damp and almost half contained mould growth. The study concluded that damp and mouldy conditions have adverse effects on symptomatic health particularly among children (see page 94).

Evidence collected by NACAB from bureaux around the country since September 1988 suggests that there has been a substantial increase in the number of homeless 16 and 17-year-olds seeking help:

> 'Once a young person is on the streets, it is very difficult to escape the downward spiral in which they are trapped. Without a home and any stability, it becomes increasingly hard to apply for, let alone sustain, a YTS place. Without such a place, there is little likelihood of obtaining any income and without any income there can be no opportunity to find somewhere to live'.[105]

The need for appropriate permanent sites and other support for travellers' children is also highlighted under this article.

The implications of full implementation of the first three paragraphs of this article for the UK are immense. Adequate monitoring must provide information to enable the standard of living of children in a complete cross-section of society to be assessed. Follow-up studies must consistently measure the effects on children of varying standards of living. Research should determine the best ways of using family support for the benefit of children currently leading impoverished lives, and social security legislation should be amended accordingly.

Article 27(4) sets out the State's obligation to ensure that parents contribute adequately to their children's maintenance. Proposed changes in legislation currently before Parliament (June 1991) are likely to make no difference in most cases to the financial situation of lone parents on income support and their children, as any maintenance received will be taken fully into account in assessing benefit. A major purpose of the legislation is to reduce the total benefit paid to lone parents, by increasing the amount of maintenance collected. Commentators have also suggested that implementation may cause additional problems for second families. Where single mothers refuse 'without good cause' to give the identity of the father, their own benefit may be reduced by up to a fifth: this will in effect punish the child or children (see also Article 2, page 4 and Article 7, page 23).

Right to education

Article 28

'1. States Parties recognize the right of the child to education, and with a view to achieving this right progressively and on the basis of equal opportunity, they shall, in particular:

(a) make primary education compulsory and available free to all;

(b) encourage the development of different forms of secondary education, including general and vocational education, make them available and accessible to every child, and take appropriate measures such as the introduction of free education and offering financial assistance in case of need;

(c) make higher education accessible to all on the basis of capacity by every appropriate means;

(d) make educational and vocational information and guidance available and accessible to all children;

(e) take measures to encourage regular attendance at schools and the reduction of drop-out rates.

2. States Parties shall take all appropriate measures to ensure that school discipline is administered in a manner consistent with the child's human dignity and in conformity with the present Convention.

3. States Parties shall promote and encourage international co-operation in matters relating to education, in particular with a view to contributing to the elimination of ignorance and illiteracy throughout the world and facilitating access to scientific and technical knowledge and modern teaching methods. In this regard, particular account shall be taken of the needs of developing countries.'

In the Convention, this and other articles had to be drafted to provide realistic targets for developing countries in which children's rights to education may be very limited. In the UK, there is a universal right to education from the beginning of the school term following a child's fifth birthday (or before in Northern Ireland, see page 31), up to the age of 19. The only children and young people who lose their basic rights to education are those who are detained in young offender institutions or prisons, or under a section of the Mental

Health Act 1983 (Education Act 1944 S.116). That minority currently has no rights under education law, although a significant number are below the minimum school leaving age of 16.

The right to education guaranteed under this article must be read in conjunction with Article 2, that is, it must be available to all children without discrimination. The article itself emphasises in its first paragraph the need for equal opportunities. Reports from Her Majesty's Inspectorate of Schools suggest that we are still far from achieving equality of opportunity. Eric Bolton, Senior Chief Inspector, noted in his second annual report: 'Sadly less able pupils are much more likely to experience the shabby and shoddy than the more able ... a worrying persistent feature of UK education at all levels'.[106]

Children and young people with disabilities and learning difficulties are still frequently refused access to ordinary schools, on the basis of compulsory assessment under the Education Act 1981. While the principle of integration is established in the Act, its fulfilment is in effect discretionary: the efficient use of resources is one criterion for denying children with disabilities an ordinary school place (Education Act 1981, S.2). There has been progress, however: children with severe learning difficulties were excluded from all rights under education legislation in England and Wales until 1971 (1975 in Scotland and 1987 in Northern Ireland). There is no obligation to make existing school buildings accessible to children with physical disabilities, although there are now access standards for new buildings (see also Article 23, page 85).

There is, in addition, direct discrimination in choice of school against children in England and Wales who get statements of special educational needs following assessment under the Education Act 1981: appeal committees hearing appeals under this Act do not have the same powers as those hearing ordinary school choice appeals under the Education Act 1980, which can direct a local education authority to admit a particular child to a school. In Scotland, the relevant appeal committees have similar rights to those hearing 'ordinary' school choice appeals.

Article 21(1)(b) says that the various forms of secondary education should be available and accessible to every child (on the basis of equal opportunity): selective (grammar) schools in certain local education authority areas are available only on the basis of selection by ability. Church schools, almost fully funded by the state, maintain control over their admissions, although they are obliged to set up appeal committees. Only discretionary financial assistance is available to help families with the real costs of 'free' schooling, which can be considerable. School uniform, compulsory in many schools (see also Article 13, page 51) can be very costly. Recent legislation (the Education Reform Act 1988) has attempted to clarify in what very limited circumstances schools are permitted to charge for activities related to education; but it seems that in many areas schools rely on 'voluntary' contributions from parents, which may discriminate against children from low-income families.

The introduction of student loans to contribute towards the cost of higher education may also discriminate against young people from families with limited means, in breach of Article 21(1)(c). According to DES statistics, the UK had the lowest full-time education participation rate for young people aged 16-18 of 13 countries, (35 per cent in 1986 against, for example, 79 per cent in the USA, and 77 per cent in Belgium and Japan). It did, however, have the second highest part-time participation rate (31 per cent against 43 per cent in Germany, and under 10 per cent in most other European countries in the study).[107] With reference to Article 28(1)(d), there are duties under the Employment and Training Act 1973 to provide vocational advice, including advice about suitable and available training and jobs, and to help pupils obtain them. Schools are obliged to publish their arrangements for careers advice as part of the information that must be made available to parents.

Education legislation to prevent school non-attendance, the subject of Article 28(1)(e), has been amended by the Children Act 1989; non-attendance in itself is no longer a ground for care proceedings, but local education authorities in England and Wales may apply for 'education supervision orders'. Under the Act, it is the supervisor's task to 'advise, assist and befriend and give directions to the supervised child and his parents in such a way as will, in the opinion of the supervisor, ensure that he is properly educated'.

Ironically, children subject to education supervision orders are the only children with a statutory right to be consulted about school choice: before giving any directions, the supervisor must, as far as reasonably practicable, 'ascertain the wishes and feelings of the child and his parents, including, in particular, their wishes as to the place at which the child should be educated', and give them due consideration (Children Act 1989, schedule 3, para. 12(2) and (3)) (see Article 12, page 46).

Concerns remain about levels of attendance, particularly in secondary schools. Monitoring is insufficient to provide the information necessary to ensure adequate implementation of this paragraph of Article 28.

Article 28(2) raises the issue of corporal punishment and other inappropriate sanctions. Legislation effectively ending corporal punishment in all state-supported education was implemented throughout the UK in August 1987. It still does not apply, however, to those pupils in independent schools whose fees are being paid by parents (many pupils in the independent sector have their fees paid wholly or partly by the State). Under the Children Act 1989, independent schools accommodating less than 50 pupils will be obliged to register as children's homes, which will bring them within the scope of regulations which prohibit physical punishment and certain other specific undesirable sanctions (see page 73). Late in 1990 the European Commission on Human Rights declared admissible the major allegations of breaches of Articles 3 and 8 of the European Convention on Human Rights (see page 188) made in two applications concerning the use of corporal punishment in independent schools.[108]

Implementation of Article 28(2), together with Article 19 (see page 69), demands the immediate extension of protection against physical punishment to all school pupils. It appears that when the Children Act is fully implemented in 1991, pupils paid for by their parents in independent schools will be the only children in institutions in England and Wales at risk of physical punishment.

In maintained schools in England and Wales, discipline is under the control of school governors and the head. There is no central direction on inappropriate sanctions beyond the legislation on corporal punishment and exclusion appeals. Full implementation demands more adequate legislation and guidance, along the lines of that applying to children's homes (see page 73). It is also essential that ethnic data on the use of various sanctions in schools should be collected, monitored and evaluated: where statistics on, for example, school exclusions have been examined on an ethnic basis, the results have suggested discrimination against certain racial groups.[109]

Article 28(3) again raises the UK's obligations to promote and encourage international efforts to improve education, in particular in developing countries, where, according to UNICEF there are 100 million children of primary school age not enrolled in school, and a further 100 million who leave without completing primary school. In 1988 the UK spent £95 million on technical cooperation in education, including £47 million provided to the British Council. Just £1.1 million of financial project aid was specifically for primary education. The UK left UNESCO, a major forum for international cooperation, in 1985.

Aims of education

Article 29

'1. States Parties agree that the education of the child shall be directed to:

(a) the development of the child's personality, talents and mental and physical abilities to their fullest potential;

(b) the development of respect for human rights and fundamental freedoms, and for the principles enshrined in the Charter of the United Nations;

(c) the development of respect for the child's parents, his or her own cultural identity, language and values, for the national values of the country in which the child is living, the country from which he or she may originate, and for civilizations different from his or her own;

(d) the preparation of the child for responsible life in a free society, in the spirit of understanding, peace, tolerance, equality of sexes, and friendship among all peoples, ethnic, national and religious groups and persons of indigenous origin;

(e) the development of respect for the natural environment.

2. No part of this article or article 28 shall be construed so as to interfere with the liberty of individuals and bodies to establish and direct educational institutions, subject always to the observance of the principles set forth in paragraph 1 of this article and to the requirements that the education given in such institutions shall conform to such minimum standards as may be laid down by the State.'

In England and Wales, major Education Acts passed in 1986 and 1988 radically altered the legal framework for the school curriculum, imposing a centrally defined National Curriculum, and increasing the powers of school governors and heads over curriculum questions outside the National Curriculum. With reference to Article 29(1)(a), the aims of the overall curriculum for maintained schools, which must be 'balanced and broadly-based', are to promote 'the spiritual, moral, cultural, mental and physical development of pupils at the school and of society' and to prepare pupils 'for the opportunities, responsibilities and experiences of adult life' (Education Reform Act, S.1).

There is no obligation in education legislation to promote human rights or the principles of the UN Charter (see Article 29(1)(b)), although amendments to this effect were proposed and debated when the Education Reform Bill (now the Education Reform Act 1989) was before Parliament. Human rights does not appear to be covered in any of the statutory orders issued for the National Curriculum (although one of the cross-curricular themes identified by the National Curriculum Council is 'Education for Citizenship', and guidance issued does suggest that 'learning about rights, duties and responsibilities is central to this component' of the curriculum; it specifically mentions the UN Convention, the European Convention on Human Rights and others[110]).

In March 1985, the Committee of Ministers of the Council of Europe recommended to member states, including the UK, that:

> 'Democracy is best learned in a democratic setting where participation is encouraged, where views can be expressed openly and discussed, where there is freedom of expression for pupils and teachers, and where there is freedom and justice ... The study of human rights in schools should lead to an understanding of, and sympathy for, the concepts of justice, equality, freedom, peace, dignity, rights and democracy. Such understandings should be both cognitive and based on experience and feelings...'[111]

The Race Relations Act 1976 is intended to eliminate unlawful racial discrimination and to promote equality of opportunity and good relations between people of different racial groups. The application of the Act to local education authorities and individual schools is considered in detail in a Code of Practice produced by the Commission for Racial Equality.[112] The development of multi-cultural education, in line with Article 29(1)(c), has not been comprehensively monitored, and there is no clear framework for it in education legislation, although there have been positive developments in individual authorities and schools. The balance proposed between development of respect for national values and for values of pupils' families' countries of origin should be reflected in primary legislation and in the detailed courses of study imposed under the National Curriculum.

Apart from provisions on education in Welsh, and on the teaching of Gaelic in Gaelic-speaking regions of Scotland (Education (Scotland) Act 1980, S.1(5) (A)(iii)), there are no legal obligations to provide education in the language spoken in a child's home, where that is not English (see also Article 30, page 119). Relevant to this, the UK is bound by a European Commission Directive on education of children of migrant workers.[113] The Directive insists that states must take appropriate steps to promote 'in co-ordination with normal education, teaching of the mother tongue and culture of the country of origin' (Article 3). Department of Education and Science (DES) responses to the European Commission about implementation of the Directive make it clear that inadequate ethnic and linguistic background data are available about children in schools to give any accurate picture: for example, the DES indicated that no figures were available for Northern Ireland. The Directive is couched in such vague language that the Commission indicated in a 1989 report on implementation it was not possible to determine if states were implementing it adequately.

The spirit of the Directive is, however, quite clear. In its report the Commission stated that in the UK:

> 'only 56 local authorities report measures to promote the teaching of the languages and culture of origin of the children of migrant workers, and even in these 56 authorities only about 6 per cent of immigrant pupils are offered integrated or deferred tuition in their language and culture of origin. The education in language and culture of origin is, furthermore, almost systematically organised outside the school (without being linked to ordinary education). The United Kingdom could therefore take steps to promote this tuition further and provide closer co-ordination with ordinary education'.[114]

It is essential that ethnic and linguistic background data are systematically collected, monitored and evaluated, together with data on teacher recruitment, training, and serving teachers, to provide information for the implementation of this article without discrimination. (A survey by the CRE of eight local education authorities found that only 2 per cent of teachers were of minority ethnic backgrounds; the average minority ethnic population of the UK is $4^1/_2$ per cent.[115]

The organisation of individual schools and colleges seldom fulfils the aims of Article 21(1)(d). The obligation to prepare pupils for 'responsible life in a free society' suggests giving them increased responsibility for their own lives in school. As the recommendation from the Committee of Ministers of the Council of Europe, quoted above, makes clear, 'democracy is best learned in a democratic setting where participation is encouraged.'

There are schools which have democratically elected school councils, but they are a small minority. It is not easy to 'teach' the values reflected in the article in a context which is authoritarian, with wide powers vested in a single person, the head teacher. In March 1984 the European Parliament adopted a resolution on freedom of education which emphasised that: 'The school system must comply with the relevant provisions of the European Convention for the Protection of Human Rights and Fundamental Freedoms'.[116]

Other current (June 1991) concerns over freedom of education have arisen over the Secretary of State for Education's decision to limit the study of history under the National Curriculum for those aged up to 14 to the period up to 1918, and for those who opt for history at 14, to the period up to the 1980s: this clearly limits many pupils' right to education about recent history and current affairs, and possibly also raises issues under Article 17 of the Convention (see page 62).

The main provisions of the Sex Discrimination Act 1975 apply to local education authorities and educational institutions, and should promote 'equality of sexes' in line with the article; the Equal Opportunities Commission continues to receive complaints about unequal access to parts of the curriculum in individual local education authorities and schools. In 1984 three 12-year-old girl pupils in Bromley successfully took their local education authority to court after they were not moved up a class at the end of the school year solely because of their sex.[117]

To a degree, the education service has reflected the growing concern over environmental issues, and aspects of the National Curriculum cover them. But there was concern early in 1991 from the Geography Association and teachers over changes made by the Secretary of State for Education in the National Curriculum *Draft Order for Geography*: with reference to environmental geography, the Secretary of State has rejected the National Curriculum Council's proposals, removing some issues dealing with 'viewpoints and attitudes'. A leading article in the *Times Educational Supplement* in January 1991 commented: 'Mr Clarke's attempts to eradicate human interests and social conflict is itself tendentious. He turns his back on the role of schools in developing children's ability to take part in decision-making in a democracy'.[118]

There is no principle in education law of promoting pupils' respect for the natural environment, and the extent to which education authorities and individual institutions themselves respect the natural environment varies widely.

Article 29(2) safeguards the right of individuals and bodies to set up educational institutions, subject to minimum state standards. The right to form independent schools remains protected by the law; the Children Act 1989 includes new provisions for England and Wales designed to ensure that children's welfare in these schools is safeguarded and promoted. The state also assists with the formation and maintenance of semi-independent voluntary schools for various established church groups – and the refusal to provide voluntary-aided status for all such groups raises issues of discrimination (see also Article 14, page 54).

Children of minorities or indigenous populations

Article 30

'In those States in which ethnic, religious or linguistic minorities or persons of indigenous origin exist, a child belonging to such a minority or who is indigenous shall not be denied the right, in community with other members of his or her group, to enjoy his or her own culture, to profess and practice his or her own religion, or to use his or her own language.'

In the UK, there is no denial by the State of the rights guaranteed by this article; the letter of the article is implemented. But the spirit of the article – and its implications in conjunction with Article 2 – demand positive encouragement and support for minority languages, cultures and religions.

The changed provisions on religious education in school in the Education Reform Act 1988 place a new emphasis on Christianity, which may well adversely affect the religious rights of minorities in schools in England and Wales (in Scotland there is no legal emphasis on Christianity). Section 7 of the Act states that the required collective worship in county (fully maintained) schools must be 'wholly or mainly of a broadly Christian character' (defined as reflecting 'the broad traditions of Christian belief without being distinctive of any particular Christian denomination'). Most, rather than all, collective acts of worship must comply, and in deciding the extent to which acts of worship will not comply, account may be taken of relevant family background and ages and aptitudes of pupils.

For children, schools devour a substantial part of their childhood, and opportunities for communal enjoyment of minority culture, religion and language should exist within schools as well as in the community, to avoid discrimination in comparison with the majority of children whose first language is English and whose religion is recognised in education legislation (see also Article 29(1)(c), page 115).

The demand for Welsh-medium education in Wales is not met by current provision, and is thus a source of discrimination: for example, in West Glamorgan three-year-olds are able to enter schooling in English-medium schools, but entry is only from four in Welsh-medium schools (and greater distances have to be travelled by many children: free transport does not apply to nursery-age education). In the same authority there is no Welsh-medium tertiary college, only a unit in a secondary school, so certain courses are only available in English. There are additional problems for children from Welsh-speaking families with special educational needs in some authorities: for instance, it appears that there has been insufficient research on speech development in Welsh-speaking children, making speech therapy provision inadequate. There is also a lack of Welsh-medium training courses for all therapies. In some areas there is no integrated provision for Welsh-medium education for children with special needs, who may have to travel long distances to attend a Welsh-medium special unit covering a variety of special needs.

The Children Act 1989 introduces a positive duty to ensure that local social services departments in England and Wales, who are looking after children (and also voluntary organisations and the proprietors of registered children's homes) must pay due regard to 'the child's religious persuasion, racial origin and cultural and linguistic background' (Children Act 1989, S. 22). The Child Care Law Review in Scotland proposes similar provisions for children in care.

Leisure, play and cultural activities

Article 31

'1. States Parties recognize the right of the child to rest and leisure, to engage in play and recreational activities appropriate to the age of the child and to participate freely in cultural life and the arts.

2. States Parties shall respect and promote the right of the child to fully participate in cultural and artistic life and shall encourage the provision of appropriate and equal opportunities for cultural, artistic, recreational and leisure activity.'

Children's rights to play are not recognised in UK legislation. Parents and other carers should take note of this article and consider whether the organisation of their home and home life provides the child with adequate play, rest and recreation.

The degree to which compulsory schooling interferes with the child's rights under this article should also be considered. In the UK children are obliged to attend school for approximately 200 days a year from the beginning of the term following their fifth birthday. This is significantly earlier than many countries in Europe and beyond: in France, Germany, Italy, Spain and Belgium primary school does not begin until six, and in Denmark seven.

Most recently in Northern Ireland, with little consultation, the compulsory school starting age has been reduced to four for many children (in the Education Reform (Northern Ireland) Order 1989, children born on or before 1 July in any year are obliged to start school in September: the youngest are therefore just four years and two months). Entry to infant school classes before the age of five is common in some education authority areas in other parts of the UK, but there is no compulsion. The appropriateness of formal, compulsory schooling for four-year-olds is at least questionable, and could well be denying them adequate play and leisure.

A report from the Policy Studies Institute, published in 1991, graphically emphasised current restrictions on children's freedom of movement:

'Over the past two decades British children have suffered a dramatic reduction in their freedom and choice to get about and do things on their own. In 1971, 80 per cent of seven and eight year-old children were allowed to go to school on their own; by 1990, this figure had fallen to nine per cent.'

Based on research into the lives of children aged 11 to 15 in five areas, the report states that while a large majority of children own bicycles, hardly any are allowed to ride on public roads and only 4 per cent of their journeys are made by bicycle. The main reasons parents give for restricting their children's independent mobility is fear of a traffic accident (and after dark the main reason is fear of 'molestation'). Parents spend a steadily increasing amount of time escorting their children; for example, three to four times as many children were taken to and from school by car in 1990 as in 1971 – and parents' use of cars adds to traffic danger and congestion. The report emphasises that the main explanation for a reduction of accidents to pedestrian children on roads is that children's mobility has been restricted.[119] The report concludes:

'The freedom gained from the growth in the ownership and use of cars has resulted in freedom lost for another sector of the community. This generation's children are being denied a whole range of opportunities for autonomy, for social development and for recreational activity that their parents and grandparents enjoyed when they were children.'

Space, facilities, and services to encourage children's play and recreation outside the home are provided at the discretion of local authorities and voluntary and private bodies. This does not implement a universal right to play and recreation without discrimination, which is implied when this Article is taken in conjunction with Article 2. Children in inner cities, in remaining high-rise blocks of flats, or crammed in 'bed and breakfast' accommodation, have little or no help from the state in finding safe space to play. A recent report from NACRO, *Growing Up on Housing Estates*, says:

'The level of social and recreational provision for children and young people on public sector housing estates in most areas is minimal. Many estates have no facilities at all ... These shortcomings have far-reaching consequences for everyone. Children are less safe. Their physical and social development can be seriously affected if they have no opportunity to play with each other'.[120]

Planners, the report suggests, 'have failed to plan for children and were principally concerned with protecting the environment from children and young people rather than including them in it'. While there has been some progress in producing safety standards for playground equipment, and guidelines from the National Playing Fields Association on playground safety, much improvement is still needed. The report refers to a survey by Play Board (replaced in 1986 by the Sports Council's National Children's Play and Recreation Unit) showing that provision of play opportunities for school-age children is patchy and uncoordinated. Play opportunities in the UK do not compare well with those in other countries.

There is, of course, a limit to the role of legislation in providing for and designing children's play: their own imagination and resources make up for many deprivations. But the lack of appropriate statutory duties clearly increases the degree of discrimination in provision for play.

With reference to out-of-school play provision, a survey by Kids Clubs Network in 1988 found there were only about 300 out-of-school care clubs in the UK, unevenly distributed around the country.[121] Three-quarters of the clubs surveyed said that the ethnic origin of their children reflected that of the local community. There is further discrimination against children with disabilities and learning difficulties whose needs for integrated play and recreation may demand special equipment. Only 43 per cent of the clubs said that children with disabilities attended: 56 per cent had wheelchair access – 40 per cent to all parts of the club.

School premises regulations insist on defined playground space. Registration of day care providers under the Children Act 1989 (covering England, Wales and Scotland) will ensure basic provision for play for those children who use the limited day care places available. Planning regulations make no specific reference to children's needs for space to play. Among a large number of proposals in the 'Declaration of the Child's Right to Play' proposed by the International Association for the Child's Right to Play is that 'adequate and appropriate space for play and recreation' should be reserved through statutory provision. The Declaration states that 'the needs of the child must have priority in the planning of human settlements', and that children and young people must be able to participate in decisions that affect their surroundings and their access to them.[122]

Article 31(2) places a clear duty on the State to 'promote' children's full participation in cultural and artistic life, and to 'encourage' the provision of 'appropriate and equal opportunities' for 'cultural, artistic, recreational and leisure activities'. There are no relevant duties in current UK legislation, and there appears to be no monitoring of the extent to which Government support for culture, arts and leisure is aimed at those aged under 18, for example, within the Arts Council budget and that of regional arts associations. As noted under Article 12 (page 48), there appears to be no representation of children's and young people's views in the arrangements for restricting admission to certain performances by age. Instrumental music tuition remains under threat in many local education authority areas. Legislation was included in the Education Reform Act 1988 clarifying when charges may be made for aspects of education provided for pupils at maintained schools. It allowed charges to be made for instrumental music tuition unless it formed part of a syllabus of a prescribed public examination, or part of the National Curriculum (with means-tested exceptions for defined low-income parents). Such legislation inevitably involves a degree of discrimination against children from poorer families. Arrangements for Local Management of Schools, coupled with financial cutbacks, have led to a number of local education authorities terminating their peripatetic music teaching service and ending the provision of instrumental music tuition to individual pupils. The Incorporated Society of Musicians wrote to local education authorities where instrumental music teaching was under threat in 1990, emphasising the need to ensure that 'all children have the opportunity to learn an instrument as a principle of general entitlement'. This article supports that principle.

Most people's definition of leisure and recreation includes the expectation of holidays away from home. Such opportunities for children living in institutions for all or much of their lives are limited and certainly not 'equal': OPCS surveys on the lives of children with disabilities found that only 55 per cent of those living in institutions had been on a special group holiday in the previous year – the majority for just one week (see also page 86).

Child labour

Article 32

'1. States Parties recognize the right of the child to be protected from economic exploitation and from performing any work that is likely to be hazardous or to interfere with the child's education, or to be harmful to the child's health or physical, mental, spiritual, moral or social development.

2. States Parties shall take legislative, administrative, social and educational measures to ensure the implementation of this article. To this end, and having regard to the relevant provisions of other international instruments, States Parties shall in particular:

(a) provide for a minimum age or minimum ages for admissions to employment;

(b) provide for appropriate regulation of the hours and conditions of employment; and

(c) provide for appropriate penalties or other sanctions to ensure the effective enforcement of this article.'

Given the definition of 'child' as anyone up to 18, UK legislation on employment does not satisfy this article, as it does not regulate the working conditions of those above 16, the age at which compulsory schooling ends (the Employment Act 1988 removed a number of existing restrictions on the employment of young people aged 16-18, although clear limits on hours of work apply to those on youth training schemes). The previous legislation was widely acknowledged to need rationalisation and simplification, but its repeal without replacement was widely criticised). The Department of Employment has indicated that the UK should make a reservation in respect of this article, because it runs contrary to the Government's policy of allowing young people aged 16 and 17 to negotiate their own terms and conditions of employment (see page 181). Time limits on much employment protection legislation (for example, having to have worked for an employer for a minimum of two years before becoming eligible) exclude those under 18.

Many commentators regard the protection against exploitation accorded to those working part-time under 16 as inadequate, and under-monitored. Basic safeguards are contained in the Children and Young Persons Act 1933 and the Children and Young Persons (Scotland) Act 1937, and local authority bylaws made under these Acts. The Employment of Children Act 1973, intended to standardise safeguards in bylaws and strengthen enforcement powers, has never been implemented.

Clearly a balance has to be struck between children's and young people's desire to work, and necessary protection from exploitation. Currently, insufficient information is collected to determine the degree of exploitation suffered by working children and young people in the UK, but surveys by non-governmental organisations give considerable cause for concern.

A National Child Employment Study carried out by the Low Pay Unit resulted in a major report 'on Britain's hidden army of child workers', early in 1991.[123] It was based on a study of almost 2,000 children aged 10-16 at a representative sample of Birmingham schools. Forty-three per cent of the children had a job (excluding babysitting, running errands and other entirely unregulated employment). One 12-year-old had three jobs – typing and answering the telephone, cleaning in a pub and helping out at a stable – taking up 19 hours a week, for which she was being paid an average of 47p an hour. Newspaper rounds are the most common jobs, accounting for 31 per cent, followed by shopwork, and cleaning.

Children themselves knew little about employment law: only 52 per cent knew that there were any restrictions at all. The Low Pay Unit suggests that three-quarters of the children were working illegally (in relation to the basic law in the Children and Young Persons Act 1933, not to the comparatively stringent bylaws operating in Birmingham). There were 203 children working under the age of 13, which is the lower age limit for part-time work. About a third of the infringements were children doing prohibited jobs, and more were working, also illegally, before 7 a.m. or after 7 p.m. Assuming that the proportion of children of secondary-school age found working illegally in this survey is a guide to what is happening throughout Birmingham, there could be 16,000 schoolchildren working illegally out of a total of approximately 20,000.

In 1988, there were only 22 convictions for offences under the employment provisions of the Children and Young Persons Act

1933. The Birmingham City Education Authority's own records show only 4,000 pupils registered as employed: 'The implication is that local education authorities are unable to administer effective legal employment of children, since this is generally registered. But illegal employment goes unrecorded, leaving the education authority powerless to act'. If the Employment of Children Act 1973 were implemented, it would oblige employers to register their intention to employ a child. At present almost all authorities require registration through their bylaws, but only when the employment has started. It can be some time before the suitability of the employment is assessed.

A similar survey of working children in the Strathclyde region of Scotland found 49 per cent of the children working illegal hours, and almost as high a proportion working in prohibited environments (such as licensed premises) or illegal jobs.[124]

Children generally earn very little. The average rate of pay found by the Low Pay Unit's survey (excluding those who received no pay at all) was £1.80 an hour. The hourly rate varied from $7^1/_2$p, earned by a 16-year-old young man who made just £1.50 for 20 hours' door-to-door selling, to £8.30, where a 13-year-old girl was paid £25 for three hours cleaning. More than half the children earned £2 an hour or less, and a quarter earned £1 an hour or less. The report concluded that 'some employers are using younger children as a cheaper alternative to older children or school leavers'. Many children are being employed in jobs which would have been subject to a minimum wage, had the Wages Act 1986 not removed entitlement for those under 18. At one school, three girls aged 14 and one aged 15 reported working in a hairdressing salon for 89p an hour, working in each case for nine hours a week.

Children at work are often at risk of injury. More than a third of the children surveyed in Birmingham reported an accident at work during the last year (and according to the Low Pay Unit, the Health and Safety Executive reported 37 serious or major accidents to children in industry or agriculture during 1989-90).

Article 7 of the Council of Europe European Social Charter (see page 193), which came into force in 1965 covers the rights of young people to protection from exploitation in employment. It provides another standard against which to measure domestic policy. Britain has declined to accept three of the ten paragraphs of Article 7: a minimum age of admission to employment of 15, apart from harmless light work; limits on working hours for those under 16 according to their needs for development and for vocational training; and at least three weeks' annual holiday with pay for those under 18. The European Commission has also been considering proposals for Europe-wide legislation to protect children and adolescents from exploitation, but so far the UK has vigorously opposed aspects of the EC Social Charter.

Economic exploitation of those under 18 is encouraged by the lack of any form of wage protection for young employees. The article should oblige the Government to review wage protection, regulation of conditions of employment of those under 18 (including health and safety), and arrangements for monitoring and enforcement.

Drug abuse

Article 33

'States Parties shall take all appropriate measures, including legislative, administrative, social and educational measures, to protect children from the illicit use of narcotic drugs and psychotropic substances as defined in the relevant international treaties, and to prevent the use of children in the illicit production and trafficking of such substances.'

Legislative protection is provided by the Misuse of Drugs Act 1971, which classifies 'controlled' drugs, and categorises drugs according to the dangers they are perceived to hold. It appears that the numbers of younger people (that is, under 20) registered as drug addicts, a tiny proportion of those using dangerous drugs, has increased over the last decade.

In relation to alcohol, there are very limited legislative controls. Children aged between five and 16 can drink alcohol on private premises. Children under 14 are not allowed in bars during licensing hours; from 14 to 16 they are allowed in but not allowed to drink alcohol; once 16, a young person may have beer, cider or perry with a meal in a bar (Licensing Act 1964), but cannot buy alcohol in a pub, shop or off-licence. A new provision in Scotland allows licensing boards to grant 'Children's Certificates' in respect of licensed premises. Where these are in force it will be permissible for a person under 14 accompanied by a person of not less than 18 to be present in licensed premises, or part of them, between 11 a.m. and 8 p.m., for the purpose of consuming a meal (Law Reform (Miscellaneous Provisions) (Scotland) Act 1990, S.49 and 50).

It is not illegal to smoke cigarettes in private at any age. If a young person aged under 16 is found smoking in a public place, tobacco and cigarette papers may be seized but not pipes or tobacco pouches (Children and Young Persons Act 1933, as amended). The Protection of Children (Tobacco) Act 1986 made it an offence to sell any product containing tobacco to those under 16. Legislation also makes it an offence to sell any substance to a person under 18 if there is reasonable cause to believe that it will be used for intoxication (Intoxicating Substances (Supply) Act 1985). There has been well-publicised concern at the lack of enforcement of this Act, and at the ease with which young children can buy cigarettes, glue and other solvents. But the problems of enforceable controls on products so readily available to adults are obvious. Legislation may be of limited value, and some would suggest it can be counter-productive.

But given the well-documented dangers of alcohol and tobacco, this article would appear to imply the need for further action to protect 16 to 18-year-olds in the UK. A recent Home Office report of the Standing Conference on Crime Prevention, *Young People and Alcohol*, suggested that 'the law regulating the consumption of alcohol by those under 18 is complicated, anomalous, and widely flouted'. [125]

The report recommended changes in legislation, banning television and cinema advertising of alcoholic drinks, and a re-examination of the Government's health education priorities 'to make them meet more closely the scale of the alcohol abuse problem'. More important, perhaps, educational measures, which are currently limited, need review: while there are voluntary agreements limiting advertising of tobacco products and alcohol, there is no prohibition. Children and young people continue to be targeted along with the adult population by those who profit from the sale of alcohol and tobacco.

Existing health education programmes may be having an effect: children are smoking less than they were a few years ago. The proportion of boys aged 11-15 smoking has fallen from 13 per cent in 1984 to 6 per cent in 1988. [126] Alcohol consumption has also fallen over the last decade. [127]

Measures to help young people addicted to drugs are under-funded and not accorded a high priority.

Sexual exploitation

Article 34

'States Parties undertake to protect the child from all forms of sexual exploitation and sexual abuse. For these purposes States Parties shall in particular take all appropriate national, bilateral and multilateral measures to prevent:

(a) the inducement or coercion of a child to engage in any unlawful sexual activity;

(b) the exploitative use of children in prostitution or other unlawful sexual practices;

(c) the exploitative use of children in pornographic performances and materials.'

While the UK certainly has a framework of legislative protection in line with this article, there are concerns about the effectiveness of state action to prevent abuse, both in the home and elsewhere. Recently there have been several cases before the courts of 'organised' sexual abuse of children by groups of adults. This may include the use of children in producing pornography, child sex rings, and ritualistic abuse: it demands a particularly coordinated approach by police, social services and other agencies, and in some cases requires close international cooperation.

'All appropriate measures' should include education to help children to protect themselves, and treatment for abusers. Many people convicted for sexual offences against children serve their term of imprisonment and are released without receiving any treatment at all. Reoffending is very common. Protection for children in institutions remains inconsistent and in some cases inadequate – for instance, in independent schools (see page 112). In recent cases proprietors and teachers at small independent schools have been found guilty of a range of serious sexual offences against pupils. Yet there is no requirement on these schools to provide access for children to an independent complaints procedure.

Sale, trafficking and abduction

Article 35

'States Parties shall take all appropriate national, bilateral and multi-lateral measures to prevent the abduction, the sale of or traffic in children for any purpose or in any form.'

Hopefully, the UK is not party to any practices which would breach this article. There has been concern that intercountry adoption has in some cases involved the sale for profit of babies from certain countries, and this practice needs urgent monitoring and control (see Article 21 page 79), both within the UK and involving international agreements (see also Article 11 page 42). There was a suggestion in a newspaper article in 1990 that some children were being 'leased' on slave contracts from parts of Africa, and that some of them had found their way to Britain, working as servants to families. [128]

Other forms of exploitation

Article 36

'States Parties shall protect the child against all other forms of exploitation prejudicial to any aspects of the child's welfare.'

This is intended to provide protection from any forms of exploitation not covered in Articles 32-35. One area of concern has been the use of children in medical research. This is not an area covered by legislation, except that any 'treatment' involving touching without a valid consent may be an assault. A draft Health Circular issued by the Department of Health in October 1989 emphasised: 'This is an especially sensitive area'. The draft stated that for all therapeutic research on those under 16, whether or not the child is judged competent to consent, consent must also be obtained from the child's parent, guardian or others acting *in loco parentis*. Furthermore:

'It should be noted that those acting for the child can only legally give their consent provided they are satisfied that the intervention is for the benefit of the child and also that their consent cannot override a refusal of consent by a child who is competent to make that decision'.

The Circular proposes that local research ethics committees should be set up to consider the ethical implications of all research proposals which involve human subjects. [129] It is too early to know whether the proposed Circular will provide adequate protection against this potential form of exploitation of children.

Torture, degrading treatment and deprivation of liberty

Article 37

'States Parties shall ensure that:

(a) No child shall be subjected to torture or other cruel, inhuman or degrading treatment or punishment. Neither capital punishment nor life imprisonment without possibility of release shall be imposed for offences committed by persons below 18 years of age;

(b) No child shall be deprived of his or her liberty unlawfully or arbitrarily. The arrest, detention or imprisonment of a child shall be in conformity with the law and shall be used only as a measure of last resort and for the shortest appropriate period of time;

(c) Every child deprived of liberty shall be treated with humanity and respect for the inherent dignity of the human person, and in a manner which takes into account the needs of persons of their age. In particular every child deprived of liberty shall be separated from adults unless it is considered in the child's best interest not to do so and shall have the right to maintain contact with his or her family through correspondence and visits, save in exceptional circumstances;

(d) Every child deprived of his or her liberty shall have the right to prompt access to legal and other appropriate assistance as well as the right to challenge the legality of the deprivation of his or her liberty before a court or other competent, independent and impartial authority and to a prompt decision on any such action.'

Article 37(a) reflects Article 3 of the European Convention on Human Rights. The UK has also accepted the European Convention for the Prevention of Torture and Inhuman or Degrading Treatment or Punishment, which came into force in February 1989, which should be considered in conjunction with this article.

There is no general prohibition on inhuman or degrading treatment and punishment in legislation controlling the treatment of children by parents or by others, but there has been progress in the last few years in limiting the use of physical punishment in institutions (see Article 19, page 69, for full discussion).

The European Commission of Human Rights has found that school corporal punishment 'may in certain circumstances amount to treatment contrary to Article 3'[130], and in a more recent case it decided that the particular use of corporal punishment did breach Article 3.[131] Legislation which has effectively ended corporal punishment in state-supported education came into effect in August 1987 throughout the UK. In independent schools, legislation against corporal punishment does not yet protect children whose fees are paid by parents rather than the state; most recently the European Commission has declared admissible applications involving beatings in independent schools alleging breaches of Article 3 and Article 8 (see Article 28(2), page 112).

To implement this article satisfactorily (together with Article 19 and Article 28(2)), for all children, the Government should review the position of children in all settings in order to provide adequate and consistent protection. Advice agencies working with children and young people do report isolated and horrifying individual cases of degrading treatment of children: being kept in their night clothes during the day in residential institutions; a child in a children's home being nailed to the floor through his shoes for three hours; a boy in a primary school having his trousers and pants lowered in front of the class by a teacher, because he was alleged to have put his hand up a girl's skirt; having family histories read out in front of other children and adults; being deprived of food and having family visits or access to siblings cancelled as part of a 'treatment' programme.

Young people on remand to prison under unruly certificates may suffer slopping out, overcrowding, long hours in cells, and bullying and intimidation from imprisoned adults. The Government proposes (under the current (June 1991) Criminal Justice Bill) to phase out remands to custody for boys aged 15 and 16 but only when sufficient 'secure accommodation' is available in the childcare system. There will be a review in four years' time. However 17-year-olds will still be held in custody.

Capital punishment was abolished for children under 16 in 1908, and for those under 18 under Section 53 of the Children and Young Persons Act 1933. (The lower limit of 18 on capital punishment is set in international instruments including the International Covenant on Civil and Political Rights (Article 6(5)). (In 1988, 30 prisoners in 14 American states were awaiting execution on death rows for crimes committed as juveniles. There have been reports of executions of young people under 18 in Pakistan, Bangladesh, Iraq and Barbados).

The sentence of life imprisonment is still available for those under 18. Under section 53(1) of the Children and Young Persons Act 1933, a person under 18 found guilty of murder must be sentenced to detention during Her Majesty's pleasure; under section 8(1) of the Criminal Justice Act 1982, those under 18 also receive a mandatory life sentence for any offence which carries a fixed life sentence in the case of an adult. The Home Secretary makes the decision about where the young person is placed and, in consultation with the Lord Chief Justice and the trial judge, when he or she should be released. In Scotland the relevant legislation refers to detention 'without limit of time', not 'imprisonment for life'.

Those sentenced under Section 53 do not come within the scope of the Parole Board (the current Criminal Justice Bill may amend this), although the Home Secretary may refer a case to the Board. In theory, a young person sentenced to life might remain in detention until he or she died.

The law on 'secure accommodation' (locked units in the childcare system) is inconsistently applied; at present the law only refers to children in care. The Government's proposals under the Children Act 1989 are that any restriction of liberty in NHS and local education authority provision, as well as residential care homes and private health institutions will be covered by the same legislation as that applying to the childcare system. The current definition of restriction of liberty does not expressly cover practices such as that termed 'Pindown', used in Staffordshire children's homes, in which young people were not locked in, but prevented from leaving by, for example putting a saucepan over the door handle. The Inquiry into Pindown has called for the revised secure accommodation regulations to make clear that such practices are defined as restriction of liberty.[132] The proposals under the Children Act do not cover independent schools or non-maintained special schools, and there will be less adequate protections outside the childcare system (on such matters as reviews and records). It is well known that 'informal' deprivation of children's liberty in schools and health institutions does occur. Some special schools have purpose-built 'time-out' rooms in which children may be placed in temporary solitary confinement (a form of inhuman and degrading treatment as well as a restriction of liberty).

Rather than trying to ensure that children who lose their liberty in these settings outside the childcare system have basic legal safeguards, the Government could have simply prohibited restriction of liberty in them – as it has done in voluntary and private children's homes.

There is no clear legislation against arbitrary restriction of liberty of children in the family home.

Article 37(b) emphasises that arrest, detention or imprisonment of children must be 'a measure of last resort and for the shortest appropriate time'. Section 53(1) of the Children and Young Persons Act 1933 provides a mandatory sentence of detention during Her Majesty's pleasure for murder: this needs amending in line with the article to ensure detention for the 'shortest appropriate time'. Under Section 53(2) of the Act (fixed sentences for other grave crimes) the court must be of the opinion that no other method of dealing with the juvenile is considered appropriate, but is not under an obligation to state in court why this is the case. Under the current (June 1991) Criminal Justice Bill those under 18 will be subject to an order for detention in a young offender institution for between two months and a year.

At present there are variable sentences for boys and girls in England and Wales, with 14-year-old boys (but not girls) eligible for custody, and boys liable to a minimum sentence of 21 days and girls a minimum of four months; such discrimination clearly breaches the Convention, and the European Convention on Human Rights, and the reforms in the current Criminal Justice Bill are designed to remedy it.

Having a prescribed minimum sentence would appear to breach the intention of this article, which is that sentences should be as short as appropriate for each individual. An argument used to defend having a defined minimum period is that the experience cannot be useful if it is too short (in fact young people do spend less time in young offender institutions if they are sentenced for breach of supervision after release).

Sentence of detention to a young offender institution is in general a sentence of last resort in that the court must be satisfied that the young person has a history of not responding to non-custodial penalties and that a custodial sentence is necessary for the protection of the public from serious harm; alternatively, detention can be imposed because the offence is so serious that a non-custodial sentence is unjustified, a condition that does not appear to fall within Article 37(b). These criteria are amended in the current Criminal Justice Bill.

The criteria for restriction of liberty in secure accommodation (to be applied to health and education establishments) do emphasise that it is to be used as a last resort. But the modified criteria for children who have been charged or convicted of a criminal offence and remanded to care (both the current criteria and those proposed for implementation under the Children Act 1989) are not justifiable under this article: for example, allowing a young person to be locked up because he ran home to his mother, even though he has every intention of attending his trial, of not interfering with justice and of not committing a crime (the reasons for adults being refused bail which are applied to juveniles).

To satisfy properly the principle that all detention of children and young people should be a last resort and for the shortest possible time, consistent legislation should apply to the various forms of detention, in each case specifying that detention must cease when the justification for it ceases to apply, coupled with an obligation to periodic and frequent review. Application of such a principle would end all punitive custody for those under 18.

The conditions and treatment of children and young people detained in secure accommodation and in young offender institutions raise issues under Article 37(c). Solitary confinement exists in many institutions. The Department of Health has produced criteria for its use in secure accommodation in community homes, but these do not apply to, for example, mental nursing homes (private health institutions) where its use is likely to be less rigorously regulated or monitored. The systematic use of solitary confinement in the Government-run St Charles Youth Treatment Centre was condemned by the Social Services Inspectorate as breaching 'acceptable ethical standards'.[133] In an application to the European Commission on Human Rights on behalf of a young man who had been detained for long periods in St Charles, the Children's Legal Centre alleged that he had been:

> 'placed in solitary confinement in a room stripped of all furniture for extensive periods – in March 1987 (when he was aged 15) for six to eight weeks and again in January 1989 (aged 16) for three weeks. During the 1987 period he was given two half-hour breaks a day for exercise, and was observed every 15 minutes, with occasional counselling from staff

members. In the 1989 period he was very cold, with two inadequate blankets, and had no exercise breaks ...'

A report from the Health Advisory Service in 1986 drew attention to the use of solitary confinement – time-out – in NHS units.[134]

In young offender institutions, the continued use of dormitory accommodation has been criticised by both the Chief Inspector of Prisons and the Coordinating Committee of Boards of Visitors, because it has led to bullying, harassment and intimidation of inmates as well as implying a loss of privacy (see also Article 16, page 58).

Juveniles are also still being remanded in police cells rather than to the care of the local authority, an entirely inappropriate form of detention which clearly breaches this article.

The right to maintain contact with family is, it appears, only legally protected for those detained in secure accommodation in community homes.

The obligation to separate those under 18 from adults in penal establishments is in practice still widely breached, although separation is Government policy. In 1989, five of the six young offender institutions for males also accommodated sentenced young adults.[135] As noted above, young people are still remanded to adult prisons (the current 1991 Criminal Justice Bill should end this practice for those aged 15 and 16. In the health service, children and young people who are detained under the Mental Health Act, and others detained as informal patients following admission by their parents, may be in wards with adult patients, although guidance suggests that they should not be. There is no obligation to separate young people from adults in mental nursing homes.

The right to prompt access to legal and other assistance for detained children, guaranteed by Article 37(d), appears to be safeguarded by legislation for those arrested and charged with criminal offences, for children in care detained in secure accommodation, and for children detained under sections of the Mental Health Act (although under the latter detention can last for up to 28 days before challenge is permitted). It is not clear whether the Government's intention is to extend similar safeguards to children not in care who may be locked up in a variety of institutions.

In 1988 Amnesty International produced a report on human rights issues arising from 'alleged forced admissions during incommunicado detention' of juveniles following arrests in connection with disturbances on the Broadwater Farm Estate in north London, in which a policeman was killed. A summary of the Amnesty report states that:

> 'detained suspects, including juveniles, were denied access to lawyers and family during lengthy periods of police interrogation ... A boy of 13 was questioned five times for a total of 15 hours, for most of the time wearing only a blanket and underpants. The judge ruled that the police had without reasonable cause refused him access to a lawyer and that 'unreasonable and unjust burdens were put on the child'. His admission was considered unreliable and he was acquitted of murder.'[136]

Children detained under a place of safety order (to be replaced from October 1991 in England and Wales by the new child protection order) frequently have their liberty restricted: there should be a clear obligation throughout the UK to ensure that they have prompt access to legal advice and assistance (as well as the right to challenge the legality of the deprivation of liberty and (see also Article 9, page 32)).

Children admitted to hospital on the authority of their parents (as 'informal' patients) may have their liberty restricted in locked wards, with no right to challenge their detention. But the Mental Health Act Commission's Code of Practice makes clear that once children are judged to have 'sufficient understanding' to make their own decisions, they cannot be kept in hospital against their will (in line with the Gillick decision[137]).

Currently (June 1991), wards of court may be locked up in secure accommodation without the right to challenge the detention. Following an application to the European Commission of Human Rights on behalf of a detained ward, the Government has undertaken to remedy this situation.

Armed conflicts

Article 38

'1. States Parties undertake to respect and to ensure respect for rules of international humanitarian law applicable to them in armed conflicts which are relevant to the child.

2. States Parties shall take all feasible measures to ensure that persons who have not attained the age of 15 years do not take a direct part in hostilities.

3. States Parties shall refrain from recruiting any person who has not attained the age of 15 years into their armed forces. In recruiting those who have attained the age of 15 years but who have not attained the age of 18 years, States Parties shall endeavour to give priority to those who are oldest.

4. In accordance with their obligations under international humanitarian law to protect the civilian population in armed conflicts, States Parties shall take all feasible measures to ensure protection and care of children who are affected by an armed conflict.'

This article places a duty on the State itself to respect, and to ensure respect by others, of international law relevant to the child. Thus, for example, the UK's role in the armed conflict with Iraq should be subject to its obligations under this article, as should the role of the armed forces in Northern Ireland.

Before the Convention was adopted in 1989, concern was expressed by the International Committee of the Red Cross (ICRC) and other organisations that the protection offered to children by this article was less than that provided by existing international instruments – in particular the Geneva Conventions and the two Additional Protocols to the Conventions.[138] Changes sought by the ICRC were not accepted, despite a petition delivered to the United Nations including the signatures of 650 youth organisations. Article 41 of the UN Convention does, however, emphasise (see page 151) that nothing in it affects provisions in the law of a state party, or in international law in force for a State, 'that are more conducive to the realization of the rights of the child'. The two additional protocols to the Geneva Conventions were adopted in 1977.

Article 77 of Protocol I, which applies to international armed conflict, provides detailed safeguards for the protection of children, including similar provisions on recruitment. Protocol II applies to non-international armed conflicts, and in Article 4 provides similar special protection for children. The UK has not yet ratified either of these additional protocols. A Parliamentary written question revealed that 97 states are party to Protocol I, and 87 to Protocol II. The UK signed both Protocols in 1977, 'but has yet to ratify them. We hope to come to a decision soon'.[139]

The minimum age of entry to the Royal Navy, Royal Marines and army is 16 for men (though, according to the Ministry of Defence 'a small number under this age are accepted'). The minimum age of entry to the Royal Air Force is $16^{1}/_{2}$, but it is planned to reduce it to 16 during 1991. The minimum age of entry for women is 17 for all services. Under-18s must have parents' or guardians' permission.

In relation to Article 38(3), there is currently no prioritisation of applicants by age; in fact some methods of recruitment – for example junior entrants and junior leaders – are specifically aimed at younger age groups. The Ministry of Defence states that there are no current plans to change policies for recruiting those under 18.

To implement this article fully, the armed services should either cease to recruit under-18-year-olds, or ensure that priority is given to recruiting the oldest among them.

The services have various age limits on overseas service, but these are not included in legislation. The minimum age in the army for service overseas is 17 years and 3 months for men; for women it is 17 and three months in Europe, and 18 elsewhere. For Northern Ireland, it is $17^{1}/_{2}$ for resident units, but no one under 18 is permitted to serve 'on the streets'. In the RAF, the minimum age for overseas service is $17^{1}/_{2}$ for men; women must have completed 12 months service. Eighteen is the minimum age for service in Northern Ireland, as it is for those in the Royal Navy and Marines. There is no minimum age for overseas service in the Navy; the minimum age for service in submarines is 17.[140] It appears that at least three 17-year-olds were killed on active service in the Falklands, and at least two in the Gulf war in 1991. In May 1991 a Select Committee of MPs reported:

'We believe that there should be at least a presumption that under-18-year-olds should not be sent on active service overseas unless there is some over-riding requirement for their particular skills in the defence of the country.'[141]

If the UK fully ratifies and observes the Additional Protocols to the Geneva Conventions, it will be able to fulfil the aims of Article 38(4). In considering our obligation to children and young people involved directly or indirectly in armed conflicts in which the UK is playing a part, like the Gulf conflict, it should be borne in mind, for example, that 48 per cent of Iraq's population is under 16.

Care for child victims

Article 39

'States Parties shall take all appropriate measures to promote physical and psychological recovery and social re-integration of a child victim of: any form of neglect, exploitation, or abuse; torture or any other form of cruel, inhuman or degrading treatment or punishment; or armed conflicts. Such recovery and re-integration shall take place in an environment which fosters the health, self-respect and dignity of the child.'

There is concern among those involved in child protection about standards of care and treatment for child victims of abuse and neglect. The Judicial Inquiry into the Cleveland child abuse affair expressed concern at the treatment of children removed from their homes following suspicion of abuse, about interviewing techniques and repeated investigations, including medical examinations.[142] The emphasis in this article is on rehabilitation and recovery. The general duties of local authorities under the Children Act 1989, to safeguard and promote the welfare of children 'in need' in their area (section 17 and part I of schedule 2), are relevant to full implementation of this article. But the Act does not specifically emphasise rehabilitation of victims. The Secretary of State has the power to add specific duties or powers (section 17(4)), and could do so in line with this article.

The present arrangements for the prosecution of alleged child abusers delay rather than promote the 'psychological recovery and social re-integration of a child victim'. Even following the reforms in the 1991 Criminal Justice Bill, children will have to attend the criminal trial of the alleged abuser to be cross examined on their evidence, which will usually be given in a video recording. Often trials take place over a year after the offences come to light and the Crown Prosecution Service routinely advises that counselling or therapy for the child should not start until after the trial for fear of tampering with the evidence. Further changes to legal procedures are necessary if the requirements of Article 39 are to be met.

Administration of juvenile justice

Article 40

'1. States Parties recognize the right of every child alleged as, accused of, or recognized as having infringed the penal law to be treated in a manner consistent with the promotion of the child's sense of dignity and worth, which reinforces the child's respect for the human rights and fundamental freedoms of others and which takes into account the child's age and the desirability of promoting the child's re-integration and the child's assuming a constructive role in society.

2. To this end, and having regard to the relevant provisions of international instruments, States Parties shall, in particular, ensure that:

(a) No child shall be alleged as, accused of, or recognized as having infringed the penal law by reason of acts or omissions which were not prohibited by national or international law at the time they were committed;

(b) Every child alleged as or accused of having infringed the penal law has at least the following guarantees:

(i) to be presumed innocent until proven guilty according to law;

(ii) to be informed promptly and directly of the charges against him or her, and if appropriate through his or her parents or legal guardian, and to have legal or other appropriate assistance in the preparation and presentation of his or her defence;

(iii) to have the matter determined without delay by a competent, independent and impartial authority or judicial body in a fair hearing according to law, in the presence of legal or other appropriate assistance and, unless it is considered not to be in the best interest of the child, in particular, taking into account his or her age or situation, his or her parents or legal guardians;

(iv) not to be compelled to give testimony or to confess guilt; to examine or have examined adverse witnesses and to obtain the participation and examination of witnesses on his or her behalf under conditions of equality;

(v) if considered to have infringed the penal law, to have this decision and any measures imposed in consequence thereof reviewed by a higher competent, independent and impartial authority or judicial body according to law;

(vi) to have the free assistance of an interpreter if the child cannot understand or speak the language used;

(vii) to have his or her privacy fully respected at all stages of the proceedings.

3. States Parties shall seek to promote the establishment of laws, procedures, authorities and institutions specifically applicable to children alleged as, accused of, or recognized as having infringed the penal law, and in particular:

(a) the establishment of a minimum age below which children shall be presumed not to have the capacity to infringe the penal law;

(b) whenever appropriate and desirable, measures for dealing with such children without resorting to judicial proceedings, providing that human rights and legal safeguards are fully respected.

4. A variety of dispositions, such as care, guidance and supervision orders; counselling; probation; foster care; education and vocational training programmes and other alternatives to institutional care shall be available to ensure that children are dealt with in a manner appropriate to their well-being and proportionate both to their circumstances and the offence.'

The general principles in Article 40(1) should be applied to all police and court treatment of children and young people suspected of and accused of criminal offences. In 1985 the United Nations General Assembly adopted the United Nations Standard Minimum Rules for the Administration of Juvenile Justice (known as the Beijing Rules). These represent detailed minimum conditions and have been accepted by the UK Government. They should be read in addition to this article, and are referred to in the Preamble to the Convention (see page 158).

While many of the basic safeguards guaranteed under this article are available throughout the UK, there are certain issues which give cause for concern. The obligation to avoid delay is breached in many individual cases in which trials and juvenile court hearings may be delayed for many months. Attempts have been made recently to limit the period of waiting for Crown Court trials (orders under the Prosecution of Offenders Act 1985 restricting the period between first appearance and committal to 70 days, and between committal and trial to 112 days, have been issued for most parts of England and

Wales, but not London or South East England). The Children Act 1989 (S.1(2)) insists that:

'in any proceedings in which any question with respect to the upbringing of a child arises, the court shall have regard to the general principle that any delay in determining the question is likely to prejudice the welfare of the child'.

A similar principle should apply to criminal proceedings involving children and young people.

With reference to Article 40(2)(b)(vi), the obligation to have an interpreter available at every stage in the criminal process is not consistently written into UK legislation applying to police investigation, arrest, detention and court proceedings.

At present, the obligation not to name those involved in criminal proceedings (the right to privacy under Article 40(2)(b)(vii)) covers 17-year-old defendants, but the current (June 1991) Criminal Justice Bill will extend this to 18.

With reference to Article 40(3)(a), the current minimum age for prosecution in England and Wales and Northern Ireland is ten, and in Scotland eight. The Children and Young Persons Act 1969 (S.4) set the minimum age for prosecution in England and Wales at 14, but this has not been implemented, and the current Criminal Justice Bill proposes to repeal it. Prosecution of those under 14 has become rarer: between 1968 and 1974, the proportion of children aged 10-13 cautioned increased from 39.1 per cent to 66.2 per cent. By 1988, 86 per cent of males and 95 per cent of females reported for an indictable offence were cautioned. Only 4,000 children under 14 were sentenced by the courts for an indictable offence in that year, and in 1989 the figure fell to 2,800. In other parts of Europe, the minimum age of prosecution is higher: 15 in Germany and Sweden, 13 in France and 12 in Portugal.

As indicated above, in England and Wales cautioning is available a an alternative to judicial proceedings, and the number of juveniles sentenced for indictable offences decreased from 90,000 in 1980 to 37,600 in 1988, a fall of 58 per cent.[143] But there is sharp regional discrimination in the use of cautioning: in 1987 the cautioning rate varied between 71 per cent and 97 per cent for boys aged 10-13, and between 28 and 83 per cent for boys aged 14-16 in different police force areas.

Research has also shown that in many areas young Black people are less likely to be cautioned than young White people, and are likely to receive fewer cautions before being taken to court (raising an issue under Article 2, read in conjunction with this article). For example, it was shown that a White juvenile with previous convictions was over four times more likely to be cautioned than his or her Black counterpart.[144] The Greater London Council's Police Monitoring Unit reported in 1982 that 40 per cent of White juveniles apprehended by the Metropolitan Police received a caution, compared with 26 per cent of Black juveniles.[145] This could not be explained by differences in the nature of the offence or previous offending history.

There are also substantial sex differences in cautioning practice. Consistent monitoring by sex and ethnic background, as well as clearer guidelines, are required to avoid discrimination. Arrangements for cautioning also vary between areas. Initially, few forces were prepared to give more than one caution. Now many forces have developed criteria for further cautions. Leicestershire Constabulary cautions a first offender by post, while most forces still administer the first caution formally at the police station. There has been concern that formal cautioning draws young people into the system who would previously have been dealt with less formally. Successive Home Office circulars have contained stronger presumptions in favour of cautioning.

Cautioning practice also raises concerns about young people's rights to privacy: some forces send a form containing details of the young person and the offence to a range of agencies including schools, social services and, in some cases, youth organisations and other voluntary organisations.

Another current concern about cautioning practice is that if a cautioned juvenile subsequently appears in court, previous cautions are generally cited, although they do not constitute a criminal record. In order to be cautioned, a juvenile must admit the offence: there are concerns that practice may encourage inappropriate admissions; citing the caution at a later court appearance may compound the problem.[146]

To implement this part of Article 40 fully, cautioning should be placed on a statutory basis, with proper guidance including consistent criteria.

In Scotland the children's hearings system provides another alternative to judicial hearings. Since the introduction of the Social Work (Scotland) Act 1968, Scotland's juvenile offenders have been regarded as requiring care rather than deserving punishment. The vast majority of offenders up to the age of 16, and some within the 16-18 age group, are diverted from the juvenile system into the children's hearings system. If the child and parents accept the grounds for referral, that he or she has committed an offence, the hearing, before three members of the public who have undergone special training, will proceed to consider whether a supervision requirement ought to be imposed. This may involve supervision of the child at home, in a foster home, or in a children's home or residential school. If the child or parents do not accept the grounds for referral, the matter must then go to the Sheriff Court for proof before the children's hearing can proceed to consider the matter. A supervision requirement imposed by a hearing does not count as a conviction, except for some limited purposes of the Rehabilitation of Offenders Act 1974.

The children's hearing system in Scotland is generally recognised as being a positive system for young offenders. There is, however, some concern that the rights of children may be abrogated in the context of a welfare system. Children have the right to obtain legal advice and assistance to prepare for a hearing or for representation at court, although they do not often take this up and are not well informed about it. They have the right to take a representative to a hearing, whose expenses will be paid, but this does not extend to the right to legal aid for a solicitor to represent them at the hearing. The Scottish Child Law Centre has heard of cases in which children have accepted grounds for referral based on 'offences' committed by them which do not in fact constitute offences. Article 40(2)(b)(iii) mentions determination of the matter in the presence of legal or other appropriate assistance. While it may be that the children's hearings system, with its ultimate recourse to the Sheriff Court, satisfies this requirement on paper, it is the experience of those involved with children that their rights are often not recognised or respected; a basic emphasis needs to be put on providing them with information and legal assistance as a matter of course.

Article 40(3) is satisfied in that there has been a growth of alternatives to custody for young offenders. The Children Act provides powers to make care, supervision and education supervision orders (building in the principles that the welfare of the child is paramount, that children's ascertainable views must be taken into account, and so on). But there are wide variations between authorities in the degree to which they use secure accommodation, and residential care rather than foster care. (It must be borne in mind that children, in particular older children, often prefer residential care to foster care, particularly when they have already experienced a number of unsatisfactory foster placements. (Further monitoring by sex and ethnic background is required to establish whether there is discrimination in relation to the use of alternatives to institutional care.)

Respect for existing standards

Article 41

'Nothing in this Convention shall affect any provisions that are more conducive to the realization of the rights of the child and that may be contained in:

(a) the law of a State Party; or

(b) international law in force for that State.'

Article 41 emphasises that the Convention must be regarded only as a baseline of minimum standards, and that it does not affect any UK domestic legislation or international instruments to which the UK is a party and which are 'more conducive to the realization of the rights of the child'.

One example is the Gillick decision: its implications are that once children are judged to have 'sufficient understanding', they should have the right to make their own decisions on important matters, unless there is some existing statute placing an age limit on self-determination (for example, the various ages of consent to sexual activity).[147] The Convention does not confer such rights of self-determination, merely of participation in decision-making under Article 12. And while Article 3 of the Convention insists that the best interests of the child shall be a 'primary' consideration, the Children Act 1989 insists that for courts determining matters concerning children's upbringing, the child's welfare must be the court's 'paramount' consideration.

Another example is the double representation of children in care proceedings, in which a guardian ad litem is appointed to represent the child's interests, and instructs a solicitor unless the child's views conflict with the guardian's. The solicitor decides whether the child has the capacity to instruct. (This important safeguard for children's rights is not, however, fully available in hearings concerning restricting a child's liberty in 'secure accommodation': in these cases the child alone instructs the solicitor, and might tell the solicitor not to oppose the application for restriction of liberty, even though the strict criteria were not met in the application. If there were an obligation to appoint a guardian as well, there could be an additional safeguard against restriction of liberty: it is accepted in international law that a person cannot validly renounce his or her own freedom.)

Our education legislation provides children and young people with much greater basic rights to receive education than the obligations of Article 28 (but as noted (page 109) there are detailed ways in which UK legislation and practice fall short of the requirements of the article).

Part II
Implementing the Convention
worldwide

Duty to inform about the Convention

Article 42

'States Parties undertake to make the principles and provisions of the Convention widely known, by appropriate and active means, to adults and children alike.'

This vital article emphasises that unless children and adults know of the rights guaranteed by the Convention, it will be of little use. It emphasises action, and also dissemination to children. Non-governmental organisations have already done much to promote knowledge of the Convention (see list of available information and teaching materials in Appendix 5, page 195). But this article places a clear duty on Government. Informing children could involve, for example, building the Convention into courses and materials that form part of the National Curriculum for England and Wales, and into advice on curriculum content for Scotland and Northern Ireland. The youth service and voluntary organisations working with children, and those parts of the media which address children directly, have obvious responsibilities. To ensure full implementation, the government will need to monitor levels of knowledge about the Convention, among all sectors of the population, including children, over the first years following ratification. There is also a duty (under Article 44, see page 177) to make widely available to the public the reports on implementation which states are obliged to submit at periods following ratification.

Effective implementation

Articles 43-45

(For full text see Appendix 1, page 176).
These articles set out the procedures for encouraging full implementation of the Convention. The Convention was adopted by the General Assembly of the United Nations on 20 November 1989 and came into force on 2 September 1990, 30 days after the twentieth country had ratified it (by June 1991, 90 states had ratified).

Committee of experts

Within six months of coming into force, each state which had ratified was able to nominate one person from among its nationals to serve on a ten-member Committee on the Rights of the Child. Election is by secret ballot of states which have ratified (states parties). Members should be 'experts of high moral standing and recognised competence in the field covered by this Convention'. There should be consideration to ensure representation of different geographical areas and legal systems. Members serve for four years, except that half the initial members will retire after two years, then elections will be held at two-yearly intervals to appoint five new members.

The Committee will normally meet annually, with the UN providing staff (the first meeting being held in summer 1991). It will submit a report on its activities every two years to the General Assembly, through the Economic and Social Council.

Reporting duty

States parties must submit a report within two years of ratifying, and thereafter every five years, 'on the measures they have adopted which give effect to the rights recognized [in the Convention] and on the progress made on the enjoyment of those rights'. Reports should contain details of 'factors and difficulties' affecting implementation, and contain sufficient information 'to provide the Committee with a comprehensive understanding of the implementation of the Convention in the country concerned'. These reports must also be made 'widely available' to the public (see also Article 42, page 154).

The Committee can request further information relevant to the implementation of the Convention from states parties.

International agencies and cooperation

The role of specialised international agencies such as UNICEF, the International Labour Organisation, the World Health Organisation, and UNESCO, are recognised. These agencies are entitled to representation when the Committee is considering the implementation of relevant articles. The Committee can ask specialised agencies to provide expert advice and submit reports.

Requests from states parties, or indications of need, for technical advice or assistance will be passed on by the Committee to UNICEF and other agencies. The Committee can also recommend to the General Assembly that the UN Secretary General should carry out particular studies. It can also make 'suggestions or general recommendations' to individual states, based on the reports it receives, reporting them also to the General Assembly together with any comments received from the state concerned.

Ratification, amendment, reservations

Articles 46 – 54

(For full text see Appendix 1, page 179).

These articles set out the procedures for ratification, entry into force, amendment of the Convention, reservations, and so on.

The Convention enters into force for a particular state 30 days after ratification. When ratifying, states may make reservations as long as they are not 'incompatible with the object and purpose' of the Convention (for details of reservations under consideration by the UK Government, see page 181). Reservations can be withdrawn at any time by notifying the Secretary-General of the UN, and withdrawal takes effect immediately.

A state can 'denounce' – that is, withdraw from – the Convention by notifying the Secretary-General in writing: this becomes effective one year later.

Any state party can propose an amendment to the Convention. The Secretary-General must circulate the amendment to states parties, asking whether they favour a conference to consider it. If within four months at least a third of states parties favour a conference, the Secretary-General must convene one: if a majority of those attending the conference approve the amendment, it will be submitted to the General Assembly for approval. The amendment will come into force if approved by the General Assembly and accepted by a two-thirds majority of states parties. It will then be binding on those states parties which have accepted it.

Appendix 1 The Convention on the Rights of the Child

Adopted by the General Assembly of the United Nations on 20 November 1989

Text

Unofficial summary of main provisions

PREAMBLE

The States Parties to the present Convention.

Considering that in accordance with the principles proclaimed in the Charter of the United Nations, recognition of the inherent dignity and of the equal and inalienable rights of all members of the human family is the foundation of freedom, justice and peace in the world,

Bearing in mind that the peoples of the United Nations have, in the Charter, reaffirmed their faith in fundamental human rights and in the dignity and worth of the human person, and have determined to promote social progress and better standards of life in larger freedom,

Recognizing that the United Nations has, in the Universal Declaration of Human Rights and in the International Covenants on Human Rights, proclaimed and agreed that everyone is entitled to all the rights and freedoms set forth therein, without distinction of any kind, such as race, colour, sex, language, religion, political or other opinion, national or social origin, property, birth or other status,

Recalling that, in the Universal Declaration of Human Rights, the United Nations has proclaimed that childhood is entitled to special care and assistance,

Convinced that the family, as the fundamental group of society and the natural environment for the growth and well-being of all its members and particularly children, should be afforded the necessary protection and assistance so that it can fully assume its responsibilities within the community,

Recognizing that the child, for the full and harmonious development of his or her personality, should grow up in a family environment, in an atmosphere of happiness, love and understanding,

Considering that the child should be fully prepared to live an individual life in society, and brought up in the spirit

PREAMBLE

The preamble: recalls the basic principles of the United Nations and specific provisions of certain relevant human rights treaties and proclamations; reaffirms the fact that children, because of their vulnerability, need special care and protection; and places special emphasis on the primary caring and protective responsibility of the family, the need for legal and other protection of the child before and after birth, the importance of respect for the cultural values of the child's community, and the vital role of international co-operation in achieving the realization of children's rights.

of the ideals proclaimed in the Charter of the United Nations, and in particular in the spirit of peace, dignity, tolerance, freedom, equality and solidarity,

Bearing in mind that the need for extending particular care to the child has been stated in the Geneva Declaration on the Rights of the Child of 1924 and in the Declaration of the Rights of the Child adopted by the United Nations in 1959 and recognized in the Universal Declaration of Human Rights, in the International Covenant on Civil and Political Rights (in particular in articles 23 and 24), in the International Covenant on Economic, Social and Cultural Rights (in particular in its article 10) and in the statutes and relevant instruments of specialized agencies and international organizations concerned with the welfare of children.

Bearing in mind that, as indicated in the Declaration of the Rights of the Child adopted by the General Assembly of the United Nations on 20 November 1959, 'the child by reason of his physical and mental immaturity, needs special safeguards and care, including appropriate legal protection, before as well as after birth',

Recalling the provisions of the Declaration on Social and Legal Principles relating to the Protection and Welfare of Children with Special Reference to Foster Placement and Adoption Nationally and Internationally (General Assembly Resolution 41/85 of 3 December 1986); the United Nations Standard Minimum Rules for the Administration of Juvenile Justice ('The Beijing Rules') (General Assembly Resolution 40/33 of 29 November 1985); and the Declaration on the Protection of Women and Children in Emergency and Armed Conflict (General Assembly Resolution 3318 (XXIX) of 14 December 1974),

Recognizing that in all countries in the world there are children living in exceptionally difficult conditions, and that such children need special consideration,

Taking due account of the importance of the traditions and cultural values of each people for the protection and harmonious development of the child,

Recognizing the importance of international cooperation for improving the living conditions of children in every country, in particular the developing countries,

Have agreed as follows:

PART I

Article 1

For the purposes of the present Convention a child means every human being below the age of 18 years unless, under the law applicable to the child, majority is attained earlier.

Definition of a child

All persons under 18, unless by law majority is attained at an earlier age.

Article 2

1. The States Parties to the present Convention shall respect and ensure the rights set forth in this Convention to each child within their jurisdiction without discrimination of any kind, irrespective of the child's or his or her parent's or legal guardian's race, colour, sex, language, religion, political or other opinion, national, ethnic or social origin, property, disability, birth or other status.

2. States Parties shall take all appropriate measures to ensure that the child is protected against all forms of discrimination or punishment on the basis of the status, activities, expressed opinions, or beliefs of the child's parents, legal guardians, or family members.

Non-discrimination

The principle that all rights apply to all children without exception, and the State's obligation to protect children from any form of discrimination. The State must not violate any right and must take positive action to promote them all.

Article 3

1. In all actions concerning children, whether undertaken by public or private social welfare institutions, courts of law, administrative authorities or legislative bodies, the best interests of the child shall be a primary consideration.

2. States Parties undertake to ensure the child such protection and care as is necessary for his or her well-being, taking into account the rights and duties of his or her parents, legal guardians, or other individuals legally responsible for him or her, and, to this end, shall take all appropriate legislative and administrative measures.

3. States Parties shall ensure that the institutions, services and facilities responsible for the care or protection of children shall conform with the standards established by competent authorities, particularly in the areas of safety, health, in the number and suitability of their staff as well as competent supervision.

Best interests of the child

All actions concerning the child should take full account of his or her best interests. The State is to provide adequate care when parents or others responsible fail to do so.

Article 4

States Parties shall undertake all appropriate legislative, administrative, and other measures, for the implementation of the rights recognized in this Convention. In regard to economic, social and cultural rights, States Parties shall undertake such measures to the maximum extent of their available resources and, where needed, within the framework of international co-operation.

Implementation of rights

The State's obligation to translate the rights in the Convention into reality.

Article 5

State Parties shall respect the responsibilities, rights, and duties of parents or, where applicable, the members of the extended family or community as provided for by the local custom, legal guardians or other persons legally responsible for the child, to provide, in a manner consistent with the evolving capacities of the child, appropriate direction and guidance in the exercise by the child of the rights recognized in the present Convention.

Parental guidance and the child's evolving capabilities

The State's duty to respect the rights and responsibilities of parents and the wider family to provide guidance appropriate to the child's evolving capacities.

Article 6

1. States Parties recognize that every child has the inherent right to life.

2. States Parties shall ensure to the maximum extent possible the survival and development of the child.

Survival and development

The inherent right to life, and the State's obligation to ensure the child's survival and development.

Article 7

1. The child shall be registered immediately after birth and shall have the right from birth to a name, the right to acquire a nationality, and, as far as possible, the right to know and be cared for by his or her parents.

2. States Parties shall ensure the implementation of these rights in accordance with their national law and their obligations under the relevant international instruments in this field, in particular where the child would otherwise be stateless.

Name and nationality

The right to have a name from birth and to be granted a nationality.

Article 8

1. States Parties undertake to respect the right of the child to preserve his or her identity, including nationality, name and family relations as recognized by law without unlawful interference.

2. Where a child is illegally deprived of some or all of the elements of his or her identity, States Parties shall provide appropriate assistance and protection, with a view to speedily re-establishing his or her identity.

Preservation of identity

The State's obligation to protect and, if necessary, re-establish the basic aspects of a child's identity (name, nationality and family ties).

Article 9

1. States Parties shall ensure that a child shall not be separated from his or her parents against their will, except when competent authorities subject to judicial review determine, in accordance with applicable law and procedures, that such separation is necessary for the best interests of the child. Such determination may be necessary in a particular case such as one involving abuse or neglect of the child by the parents, or one where the parents are living separately and a decision must be made as to the child's place of residence.

Separation from parents

The child's right to live with his/her parents unless this is deemed incompatible with his/her best interests; the right to maintain contact with both parents if separated from one or both; the duties of States in cases where such separation results from State action.

2. In any proceedings pursuant to paragraph 1, all interested parties shall be given an opportunity to participate in the proceedings and make their views known.

3. States Parties shall respect the right of the child who is separated from one or both parents to maintain personal relations and direct contact with both parents on a regular basis, except if it is contrary to the child's best interests.

4. Where such separation results from any action initiated by a State Party, such as the detention, imprisonment, exile, deportation or death (including death arising from any cause while the person is in the custody of the State) of one or both parents or of the child, that State Party shall, upon request, provide the parents, the child or, if appropriate, another member of the family with the essential information concerning the whereabouts of the absent member(s) of the family unless the provision of the information would be detrimental to the well-being of the child. States Parties shall further ensure that the submission of such a request shall of itself entail no adverse consequences for the person(s) concerned.

Article 10

Family reunification

1. In accordance with the obligation of States Parties under article 9, paragraph 1, applications by a child or his or her parents to enter or leave a State Party for the purpose of family reunification shall be dealt with by States Parties in a positive, humane, and expeditious manner. States Parties shall further ensure that the submission of such a request shall entail no adverse consequences for the applicants and for the members of their family.

The right of children and their parents to leave any country and to enter their own in order to be reunited or to maintain the child-parent relationship.

2. A child whose parents reside in different States shall have the right to maintain on a regular basis save in exceptional circumstances personal relations and direct contacts with both parents. Towards that end and in accordance with the obligation of States Parties under article 9, paragraph 2, States Parties shall respect the right of the child and his or her parents to leave any country, including their own, and to enter their own country. The right to leave any country shall be subject only to such restrictions as are prescribed by law and which are necessary to protect the national security, public order (*ordre public*), public health or morals or the rights and freedoms of others and are consistent with the other rights recognized in the present Convention.

Article 11

Illicit transfer and non-return

1. States Parties shall take measures to combat the illicit transfer and non-return of children abroad.

The State's obligation to try to prevent and remedy the kidnapping or retention of children abroad by a parent or third party.

2. To this end, States Parties shall promote the conclusion of bilateral or multilateral agreements or accession to existing agreements.

Article 12

1. States Parties shall assure to the child who is capable of forming his or her own views the right to express those views freely in all matters affecting the child, the views of the child being given due weight in accordance with the age and maturity of the child.

2. For this purpose, the child shall in particular be provided the opportunity to be heard in any judicial and administrative proceedings affecting the child, either directly, or through a representative or an appropriate body, in a manner consistent with the procedural rules of national law.

The child's opinion

The child's right to express an opinion, and to have that opinion taken into account, in any matter or procedure affecting the child.

Article 13

1. The child shall have the right to freedom of expression: this right shall include freedom to seek, receive and impart information and ideas of all kinds, regardless of frontiers, either orally, in writing or in print, in the form of art, or through any other media of the child's choice.

2. The exercise of this right may be subject to certain restrictions, but these shall only be such as are provided by law and are necessary:

a) for respect of the rights or reputations of others: or

b) for the protection of national security or of public order (*ordre public*), or of public health or morals.

Freedom of expression

The child's right to obtain and make known information, and to express his or her views, unless this would violate the rights of others.

Article 14

1. States Parties shall respect the right of the child to freedom of thought, conscience and religion.

2. States Parties shall respect the rights and duties of the parents and, when applicable, legal guardians, to provide direction to the child in the exercise of his or her right in a manner consistent with the evolving capacities of the child.

3. Freedom to manifest one's religion or beliefs may be subject only to such limitations as are prescribed by law and are necessary to protect public safety, order, health, or morals or the fundamental rights and freedoms of others.

Freedom of thought, conscience and religion

The child's right to freedom of thought, conscience and religion, subject to appropriate parental guidance and national law.

Article 15

1. States Parties recognize the rights of the child to freedom of association and to freedom of peaceful assembly.

Freedom of association

2. No restrictions may be placed on the exercises of these rights other than those imposed in conformity with the law and which are necessary in a democratic society in the interest of national security or public safety, public order (*ordre public*), the protection of public health or morals or the protection of the rights and freedoms of others.

The right of children to meet with others and to join or set up associations, unless the fact of doing so violates the rights of others.

Article 16

1. No child shall be subjected to arbitrary or unlawful interference with his or her privacy, family, home or correspondence, nor to unlawful attacks on his or her honour and reputation.

2. The child has the right to the protection of the law against such interference or attacks.

Protection of privacy

The right to protection from interference with privacy, family, home and correspondence, and from libel/slander.

See also Article 37 and young offender's institutions.

Article 17

States Parties recognise the important function performed by the mass media and shall ensure that the child has access to information and material from a diversity of national and international sources, especially those aimed at the promotion of his or her social, spiritual and moral well-being and physical and mental health. To this end, States Parties shall:

a) Encourage the mass media to disseminate information and material of social and cultural benefit to the child and in accordance with the spirit of article 29;

b) Encourage international co-operation in the production, exchange and dissemination of such information and material from a diversity of cultural, national and international sources;

c) Encourage the production and dissemination of children's books;

d) Encourage the mass media to have particular regard to the linguistic needs of the child who belongs to a minority group or who is indigenous;

e) Encourage the development of appropriate guidelines for the protection of the child from information and material injurious to his or her well-being bearing in mind the provisions of articles 13 and 18.

Access to appropriate information

The role of the media in disseminating information to children that is consistent with moral well-being and knowledge and understanding among peoples, and respects the child's cultural background. The State is to take measures to encourage this and to protect children from harmful materials.

Article 18

1. States Parties shall use their best efforts to ensure recognition of the principle that both parents have common responsibilities for the upbringing and development of the child. Parents or, as the case may be, legal guardians, have the primary responsibility for the upbringing and development of the child. The best interests of the child will be their basic concern.

Parental responsibilities

The principle that both parents have joint primary responsibility for bringing up their children, and that the State should support them in this task.

2. For the purpose of guaranteeing and promoting the rights set forth in this Convention, States Parties shall render appropriate assistance to parents and legal guardians in the performance of their child-rearing responsibilities and shall ensure the development of institutions, facilities and services for the care of children.

3. States Parties shall take all appropriate measures to ensure that children of working parents have the right to benefit from child care services and facilities for which they are eligible.

Article 19

1. States Parties shall take all appropriate legislative, administrative, social and educational measures to protect the child from all forms of physical or mental violence, injury or abuse, neglect or negligent treatment, maltreatment or exploitation including sexual abuse, while in the care of parent(s), legal guardian(s) or any other person who has the care of the child.

2. Such protective measures should, as appropriate, include effective procedures for the establishment of social programmes to provide necessary support for the child and for those who have the care of the child, as well as for other forms of prevention and for identification, reporting, referral, investigation, treatment, and follow-up of instances of child maltreatment described heretofore, and, as appropriate, for judicial involvement.

Protection from abuse and neglect

The State's obligation to protect children from all forms of maltreatment perpetrated by parents or others responsible for their care, and to undertake preventive and treatment programmes in this regard.

Article 20

1. A child temporarily or permanently deprived of his or her family environment or in whose own best interests cannot be allowed to remain in that environment, shall be entitled to special protection and assistance provided by the State.

2. State Parties shall in accordance with their national laws ensure alternative care for such a child.

3. Such care should include, *inter alia*, foster placement, Kafala of Islamic law, adoption, or if necessary placement in suitable institutions for the care of children. When considering solutions, due regard shall be paid to the desirability of continuity in a child's upbringing and to the child's ethnic, religious, cultural and linguistic background.

Protection of children without families

The State's obligation to provide special protection for children deprived of their family environment and to ensure that appropriate alternative family care or institutional placement is made available to them, taking into account the child's cultural background.

Article 21

Adoption

States Parties which recognize and/or permit the system of adoption shall ensure that the best interests of the child shall be the paramount consideration and they shall:

In countries where adoption is recognized and/or allowed, it shall only be carried out in the best interests of the child, with all necessary safeguards for a given child and authorization by the competent authorities.

a) ensure that the adoption of a child is authorized only by competent authorities who determine, in accordance with applicable law and procedures and on the basis of all pertinent and reliable information, that the adoption is permissible in view of the child's status concerning parents, relatives and legal guardians and that, if required, the persons concerned have given their informed consent to the adoption on the basis of such counselling as may be necessary;

b) recognize that intercountry adoption may be considered as an alternative means of child's care, if the child cannot be placed in a foster or an adoptive family or cannot in any suitable manner be cared for in the child's country of origin;

c) ensure that the child concerned by intercountry adoption enjoys safeguards and standards equivalent to those existing in the case of national adoption;

d) take all appropriate measures to ensure that, in intercountry adoption, the placement does not result in improper financial gain for those involved in it;

e) promote, where appropriate, the objectives of this article by concluding bilateral or multilateral arrangements or agreements, and endeavour, within this framework, to ensure that the placement of the child in another country is carried out by competent authorities or organs.

Article 22

Refugee children

1. States Parties shall take appropriate measures to ensure that a child who is seeking refugee status or who is considered a refugee in accordance with applicable international or domestic law and procedures shall, whether unaccompanied or accompanied by his or her parents or by any other person, receive appropriate protection and humanitarian assistance in the enjoyment of applicable rights set forth in this Convention and in other international human rights or humanitarian instruments to which the said States are Parties.

Special protection to be granted to children who are refugees or seeking refugee status, and the State's obligation to co-operate with competent organizations providing such protection and assistance.

2. For this purpose, States Parties shall provide, as they consider appropriate, co-operation in any efforts by the United Nations and other competent intergovernmental organizations or non-governmental organizations co-operating with the United Nations to protect and assist

such a child to trace the parents or other members of the family of any refugee child in order to obtain information necessary for reunification with his or her family. In cases where no parents or other members of the family can be found, the child shall be accorded the same protection as any other child permanently or temporarily deprived of his or her family environment for any reason, as set forth in the present Convention.

Article 23

Handicapped children

1. States Parties recognize that a mentally or physically disabled child should enjoy a full and decent life, in conditions which ensure dignity, promote self-reliance, and facilitate the child's active participation in the community.

The right of handicapped children to special care, education and training designed to help them to achieve greatest possible self-reliance and to lead a full and active life in society.

2. States Parties recognize the right of the disabled child to special care and shall encourage and ensure the extension, subject to available resources, to the eligible child and those responsible for his or her care, of assistance for which application is made and which is appropriate to the child's condition and to the circumstances of the parents or others caring for the child.

3. Recognizing the special needs of a disabled child, assistance extended in according with paragraph 2 shall be provided free of charge, whenever possible, taking into account the financial resources of the parents or others caring for the child, and shall be designed to ensure that the disabled child has effective access to and receives education, training, health care services, rehabilitation services, preparation for employment and recreation opportunities in a manner conducive to the child's achieving the fullest possible social integration and individual development, including his or her cultural and spiritual development.

4. States Parties shall promote in the spirit of international co-operation the exchange of appropriate information in the field of preventive health care and of medical, psychological and functional treatment of disabled children, including dissemination of and access to information concerning methods of rehabilitation education and vocational services, with the aim of enabling States Parties to improve their capabilities and skills and to widen their experience in these areas. In this regard, particular account shall be taken of the needs of developing countries.

Article 24

1. States Parties recognize the right of the child to the enjoyment of the highest attainable standard of health and to facilities for the treatment of illness and rehabilitation of health. States Parties shall strive to ensure that no child is deprived of his or her right of access to such health care services.

2. States Parties shall pursue full implementation of this right and, in particular, shall take appropriate measures:

a) to diminish infant and child mortality;

b) to ensure the provision of necessary medical assistance and health care to all children with emphasis on the development of primary health care;

c) to combat disease and malnutrition including within the framework of primary health care, through *inter alia* the application of readily available technology and through the provision of adequate nutritious foods and clean drinking water, taking into consideration the dangers and risks of environmental pollution;

d) to ensure appropriate pre- and post-natal care for mothers;

e) to ensure that all segments of society, in particular parents and children, are informed, have access to education and are supported in the use of, basic knowledge of child health and nutrition, the advantages of breast-feeding, hygiene and environmental sanitation and the prevention of accidents;

f) to develop preventive health care, guidance for parents, and family planning education and services.

3. States Parties shall take all effective and appropriate measures with a view to abolishing traditional practices prejudicial to the health of children.

4) States Parties undertake to promote and encourage international co-operation with a view to achieving progressively the full realization of the right recognized in this article. In this regard, particular account shall be taken of the needs of developing countries.

Health and health services

The right to the highest level of health possible and to access to health and medical services, with special emphasis on primary and preventive health care, public health education and the diminution of infant mortality. The State's obligation to work towards the abolition of harmful traditional practices. Emphasis is laid on the need for international co-operation to ensure this right.

Article 25

States Parties recognize the right of a child who has been placed by the competent authorities for the purposes of care, protection, or treatment of his or her physical or mental health, to a periodic review of the treatment provided to the child and all other circumstances relevant to his or her placement.

Periodic review of placement

The right of children placed by the State for reasons of care, protection or treatment to have all aspects of that placement evaluated regularly.

Article 26

1. States Parties shall recognize for every child the right to benefit from social security, including social insurance, and shall take the necessary measures to achieve the full realization of this right in accordance with their national law.

2. The benefits should, where appropriate, be granted taking into account the resources and the circumstances of the child and persons having responsibility for the maintenance of the child as well as any other consideration relevant to an application for benefits made by or on behalf of the child.

Social security

The right of children to benefit from social security.

Article 27

1. States Parties recognize the right of every child to a standard of living adequate for the child's physical, mental, spiritual, moral and social development.

2. The parent(s) or others responsible for the child have the primary responsibility to secure, within their abilities and financial capacities, the conditions of living necessary for the child's development.

3. States Parties in accordance with national conditions and within their means shall take appropriate measures to assist parents and others responsible for the child to implement this right and shall in case of need provide material assistance and support programmes, particularly with regard to nutrition, clothing and housing.

4. States Parties shall take all appropriate measures to secure the recovery of maintenance for the child from the parents or other persons having financial responsibility for the child, both within the State Party and from abroad. In particular, where the person having financial responsibility for the child lives in a State different from that of the child. States Parties shall promote the accession to international agreements or the conclusion of such agreements as well as the making of other appropriate arrangements.

Standard of living

The right of children to benefit from an adequate standard of living, the primary responsibility to provide this and the State's duty to ensure that this responsibility is first fulfillable and then fulfilled, where necessary through the recovery of maintenance.

Article 28

1. State Parties recognize the right of the child to education, and with a view to achieving this right progressively and on the basis of equal opportunity, they shall, in particular:

a) make primary education compulsory and available free to all;

b) encourage the development of different forms of secondary education, including general and vocational education, make them available and accessible to every child, and take appropriate measures such as the introduction of free education and offering financial assistance in case of need;

c) make higher education accessible to all on the basis of capacity by every appropriate means;

d) make educational and vocational information and guidance available and accessible to all children;

e) take measures to encourage regular attendance at schools and the reduction of drop-out rates.

2. States Parties shall take all appropriate measures to ensure that school discipline is administered in a manner consistent with the child's human dignity and in conformity with the present Convention.

3. States Parties shall promote and encourage international co-operation in matters relating to education, in particular with a view to contributing to the elimination of ignorance and illiteracy throughout the world and facilitating access to scientific and technical knowledge and modern teaching methods. In this regard, particular account shall be taken of the needs of developing countries.

Education

The child's right to education, and the State's duty to ensure that primary education at least is made free and compulsory. Administration of school discipline is to reflect the child's human dignity. Emphasis is laid on the need for international co-operation to ensure this right.

Article 29

1. States Parties agree that the education of the child shall be directed to:

a) the development of the child's personality, talents and mental and physical abilities to their fullest potential;

b) the development of respect for human rights and fundamental freedoms, and for the principles enshrined in the Charter of the United Nations;

c) the development of respect for the child's parents, his or her own cultural identity, language and values, for the national values of the country in which the child is living, the country from which he or she may originate, and for civilizations different from his or her own;

Aims of education

The State's recognition that education should be directed at developing the child's personality and talents, preparing the child for active life as an adult, fostering respect for basic human rights and developing respect for the child's own cultural and national values and those of others.

d) the preparation of the child for responsible life in a free society, in the spirit of understanding, peace, tolerance, equality of sexes, and friendship among all peoples, ethnic, national and religious groups and persons of indigenous origin;

e) the development of respect for the natural environment.

2. No part of this article or article 28 shall be constructed so as to interfere with the liberty of individuals and bodies to establish and direct educational institutions, subject always to the observance of the principles set forth in paragraph 1 of this article and to the requirements that the education given in such institutions shall conform to such minimum standards as may be laid down by the State.

Article 30

In those States in which ethnic, religious or linguistic minorities or persons of indigenous origin exist, a child belonging to such a minority or who is indigenous shall not be denied the right, in community with other members of his or her group, to enjoy his or her own culture, to profess and practice his or her own religion, or to use his or her own language.

Children of minorities or indigenous populations

The right of children of minority communities and indigenous populations to enjoy their own culture and to practice their own religion and language.

Article 31

1. States Parties recognize the right of the child to rest and leisure, to engage in play and recreational activities appropriate to the age of the child and to participate freely in cultural life and the arts.

2. States Parties shall respect and promote the right of the child to fully participate in cultural and artistic life and shall encourage the provision of appropriate and equal opportunities for cultural, artistic, recreational and leisure activity.

Leisure, recreation and cultural activities

The right of children to leisure, play and participation in cultural and artistic activities.

Article 32

1. States Parties recognize the right of the child to be protected from economic exploitation and from performing any work that is likely to be hazardous or to interfere with the child's education, or to be harmful to the child's health or physical, mental, spiritual, moral or social development.

2. States Parties shall take legislative, administrative, social and educational measures to ensure the implementation of this article. To this end, and having regard to the relevant provisions of other international instruments, States Parties shall in particular:

Child labour

The State's obligation to protect children from engaging in work that constitutes a threat to their health, education or development, to set minimum ages for employment, and to regulate conditions of employment.

a) provide for a minimum age or minimum ages for admissions to employment;

b) provide for appropriate regulation of the hours and conditions of employment; and

c) provide for appropriate penalties or other sanctions to ensure the effective enforcement of this article.

Article 33

States Parties shall take all appropriate measures, including legislative, administrative, social and educational measures, to protect children from the illicit use of narcotic drugs and psychotropic substances as defined in the relevant international treaties, and to prevent the use of children in the illicit production and trafficking of such substances.

Drug abuse

The child's right to protection from the use of narcotic and psychotropic drugs and from being involved in their production or distribution.

Article 34

States Parties undertake to protect the child from all forms of sexual exploitation and sexual abuse. For these purposes States Parties shall in particular take all appropriate national, bilateral and multilateral measures to prevent:

Sexual exploitation

The child's right to protection from sexual exploitation and abuse, including prostitution and involvement in pornography.

a) the inducement or coercion of a child to engage in any unlawful sexual activity;

b) the exploitative use of children in prostitution or other unlawful sexual practices;

c) the exploitative use of children in pornographic performances and materials.

Article 35

States Parties shall take all appropriate national, bilateral and multilateral measures to prevent the abduction, the sale of or traffic in children for any purpose or in any form.

Sale, trafficking and abduction

The State's obligation to make every effort to prevent the sale, trafficking and abduction of children.

Article 36

States Parties shall protect the child against all other forms of exploitation prejudicial to any aspects of the child's welfare.

Other forms of exploitation

The child's right to protection from all other forms of exploitation not covered in articles 32, 33, 34 and 35.

Article 37

States Parties shall ensure that:

a) No child shall be subjected to torture or other cruel, inhuman or degrading treatment or punishment. Neither capital punishment nor life imprisonment without possibility of release shall be imposed for offences committed by persons below 18 years of age;

b) No child shall be deprived of his or her liberty unlawfully or arbitrarily. The arrest, detention or imprisonment of a child shall be in conformity with the law and shall be used only as a measure of last resort and for the shortest appropriate period of time;

c) Every child deprived of liberty shall be treated with humanity and respect for the inherent dignity of the human person, and in a manner which takes into account the needs of persons of their age. In particular every child deprived of liberty shall be separated from adults unless it is considered in the child's best interest not to do so and shall have the right to maintain contact with is or her family through correspondence and visits, and save in exceptional circumstances;

d) Every child deprived of his or her liberty shall have the right to prompt access to legal and other appropriate assistance as well as the right to challenge the legality of the deprivation of his or her liberty before a court or other competent, independent and impartial authority and to a prompt decision on any such action.

Torture and deprivation of liberty

The prohibition of torture, cruel treatment or punishment, capital punishment, life imprisonment, and unlawful arrest or deprivation of liberty. The principles of appropriate treatment, separation from detained adults, contact with family and access to legal and other assistance.

Article 38

1. States Parties undertake to respect and to ensure respect for rules of international humanitarian law applicable to them in armed conflicts which are relevant to the child.

2. States Parties shall take all feasible measures to ensure that persons who have not attained the age of 15 years do not take a direct part in hostilities.

3. States Parties shall refrain from recruiting any person who has not attained the age of 15 years into their armed forces. In recruiting among those persons who have attained the age of 15 years but who have not attained the age of 18 years, States Parties shall endeavour to give priority to those who are oldest.

4. In accordance with their obligations under international humanitarian law to protect the civilian population in armed conflicts, States Parties shall take all feasible measures to ensure protection and care of children who are affected by an armed conflict.

Armed conflicts

The obligation of States to respect and ensure respect for humanitarian law as it applies to children. The principle that no child under 15 take a direct part in hostilities or be recruited into the armed forces, and that all children affected by armed conflict benefit from protection and care.

Article 39

States Parties shall take all appropriate measures to promote physical and psychological recovery and social re-integration of a child victim of: any form of neglect, exploitation, or abuse; torture or any other form of cruel, inhuman or degrading treatment or punishment; or armed conflicts. Such recovery and re-integration shall take place in an environment which fosters the health, self-respect and dignity of the child.

Article 40

1. States Parties recognize the right of every child alleged as, accused of, or recognized as having infringed the penal law to be treated in a manner consistent with the promotion of the child's sense of dignity and worth, which reinforces the child's respect for the human rights and fundamental freedoms of others and which takes into account the child's age and the desirability of promoting the child's re-integration and the child's assuming a constructive role in society.

2. To this end, and having regard to the relevant provisions of international instruments, States Parties shall, in particular, ensure that:

a) No child shall be alleged as, be accused of, or recognized as having infringed the penal law by reason of acts or omissions which were not prohibited by national or international law at the time they were committed;

b) Every child alleged as or accused of having infringed the penal law has at least the following guarantees:

i   to be presumed innocent until proven guilty according to law;

ii to be informed promptly and directly of the charges against him or her, and if appropriate through his or her parents or legal guardian, and to have legal or other appropriate assistance in the preparation and presentation of his or her defence;

iii to have the matter determined without delay by a competent, independent and impartial authority or judicial body in a fair hearing according to law, in the presence of legal or other appropriate assistance and, unless it is considered not to be in the best interest of the child, in particular, taking into account his or her age or situation, his or her parents or legal guardians:

iv not to be compelled to give testimony or to confess guilt; to examine or have examined adverse witnesses and to obtain the participation and examination of witnesses on his or her behalf under conditions of equality;

Rehabilitative care

The State's obligation to ensure that child victims of armed conflicts, torture, neglect, maltreatment or exploitation receive appropriate treatment for their recovery and social re-integration.

Administration of juvenile justice

The right of children alleged or recognized as having committed an offence to respect for their human rights and, in particular, to benefit from all aspects of the due process of law, including legal or other assistance in preparing and presenting their defence. The principle that recourse to judicial proceedings and institutional placements should be avoided wherever possible and appropriate.

v   if considered to have infringed the penal law, to have this decision and any measures imposed in consequence thereof reviewed by a higher competent, independent and impartial authority or judicial body according to law;

vi to have the free assistance of an interpreter if the child cannot understand or speak the language used;

vii to have his or her privacy fully respected at all stages of the proceedings.

3. States Parties shall seek to promote the establishment of laws, procedures, authorities and institutions specifically applicable to children alleged as, accused of, or recognized as having infringed the penal law, and in particular:

a) the establishment of a minimum age below which children shall be presumed not to have the capacity to infringe the penal law;

b) whenever appropriate and desirable, measures for dealing with such children without resorting to judicial proceedings, providing that human rights and legal safeguards are fully respected.

4. A variety of dispositions, such as care, guidance and supervision orders; counselling; probation; foster care; education and vocational training programmes and other alternatives to institutional care shall be available to ensure that children are dealt with in a manner appropriate to their well-being and proportionate both to their circumstances and the offence.

Article 41

Nothing in this Convention shall affect any provisions that are more conducive to the realization of the rights of the child and that may be contained in:

a)the law of a State Party; or

b)international law in force for that State.

Respect for existing standards

The principle that if any standards set in national law or other applicable international instruments are higher than those of this Convention, it is the higher standard that applies.

PART II

Article 42

States Parties undertake to make the principles and provisions of the Convention widely known, by appropriate and active means, to adults and children alike.

Article 43

1. For the purpose of examining the progress made by States Parties in achieving the realization of the obligations undertaken in the present Convention, there shall be established a Committee on the Rights of the Child, which shall carry out the functions hereinafter provided.

2. The Committee shall consist of 10 experts of high moral standing and recognized competence in the field covered by this Convention. The members of the Committee shall be elected by States Parties from among their nationals and shall serve in their personal capacity, consideration being given to equitable geographical distribution as well as to the principal legal systems.

3. The members of the Committee shall be elected by secret ballot from a list of persons nominated by States Parties. Each State Party may nominate one person from among its own nationals.

4. The initial election to the Committee shall be held no later than six months after the date of the entry into force of the present Convention and thereafter every second year. At least four months before the date of each election, the Secretary-General of the United Nations shall address a letter to States Parties inviting them to submit their nominations within two months. The Secretary-General shall subsequently prepare a list in alphabetical order of all persons thus nominated, indicating States Parties which have nominated them, and shall submit it to the States Parties to the present Convention.

5. The elections shall be held at meetings of States Parties convened by the Secretary-General at United Nations Headquarters. At those meetings, for which two-thirds of States Parties shall constitute a quorum, the persons elected to the Committee shall be those who obtain the largest number of votes and an absolute majority of the votes of the representatives of States Parties present and voting.

Implementation and entry into force

The provisions of articles 42-54 notably foresee:

i) the State's obligation to make the rights contained in this Convention widely known to both adults and children.

ii) the setting up of a Committee on the Rights of the Child composed of ten experts, which will consider reports that States Parties to the Convention are to submit two years after ratification and every five years thereafter.

iii) States Parties are to make their reports widely available to the general public.

iv) The Committee may propose that special studies be undertaken on specific issues relating to the rights of the child, and may make its evaluations known to each State Party concerned as well as to the UN General Assembly.

v) In order to 'foster the effective implementation of the Convention and to encourage international co-operation', the specialized agencies of the UN (such as the ILO, WHO and UNESCO) and UNICEF would be able to attend the meetings of the Committee. Together with any other body recognised as 'competent', including NGOs in consultative status with the UN and UN organs such as the UNHCR, they can submit pertinent information to the Committee and be asked to advise on the optimal implementation of the Convention.

6. The members of the Committee shall be elected for a term of four years. They shall be eligible for re-election if renominated. The term of five of the members elected at the first election shall expire at the end of two years; immediately after the first election the names of these five members shall be chosen by lot by the Chairman of the meeting.

7. If a member of the Committee dies or resigns or declares that for any other cause he or she can no longer perform the duties of the Committee, the State Party which nominated the member shall appoint another expert from among its nationals to serve for the remainder of the term, subject to the approval of the Committee.

8. The Committee shall establish its own rules of procedure.

9. The Committee shall elect its officers for a period of two years.

10. The meetings of the Committee shall normally be held at the United Nations Headquarters or at any other convenient place as determined by the Committee. The Committee shall normally meet annually. The duration of the meetings of the Committee shall be determined, and reviewed, if necessary, by a meeting of the States Parties to the present Convention, subject to the approval of the General Assembly.

11. The Secretary-General of the United Nations shall provide the necessary staff and facilities for the effective performance of the functions of the Committee under the present Convention.

12. With the approval of the General Assembly, the members of the Committee established under the present Convention shall receive emoluments from the United Nations resources on such terms and conditions as the Assembly may decide.

Article 44

1. States Parties undertake to submit to the Committee, through the Secretary-General of the United Nations, reports on the measures they have adopted which give effect to the rights recognized herein and on the progress made on the enjoyment of those rights:

a) within two years of the entry into force of the Convention for the State Party concerned,

b) thereafter every five years.

2. Reports made under this article shall indicate factors and difficulties, if any, affecting the degree of fulfilment of the obligations under the present Convention. Reports shall also contain sufficient information to provide the Committee with a comprehensive understanding of the implementation of the Convention in the country concerned.

3. A State Party which has submitted a comprehensive initial report to the Committee need not in its subsequent reports submitted in accordance with paragraph 1(b) repeat basic information previously provided.

4. The Committee may request from States Parties further information relevant to the implementation of the Convention.

5. The Committee shall submit to the General Assembly of the United Nations through the Economic and Social Council, every two years, reports on its activities.

6. States Parties shall make their reports widely available to the public in their own countries.

Article 45

In order to foster the effective implementation of the Convention and to encourage international co-operation in the field covered by the Convention:

a) The specialized agencies, UNICEF and other United Nations organs shall be entitled to be represented at the consideration of the implementation of such provisions of the present Convention as fall within the scope of their mandate. The Committee may invite the specialized agencies, UNICEF and other competent bodies as it may consider appropriate to provide expert advice on the implementation of the Convention in areas falling within the scope of their respective mandates. The Committee may invite the specialized agencies, UNICEF and other United Nations organs to submit reports on the implementation of the Convention in areas falling within the scope of their activities.

b) The Committee shall transmit, as it may consider appropriate, to the specialized agencies, UNICEF and other competent bodies, any reports from States Parties that contain a request, or indicate a need, for technical advice or assistance along with the Committee's observations and suggestions, if any, on these requests or indications.

c) The Committee may recommend to the General Assembly to request the Secretary-General to undertake on its behalf studies on specific issues relating to the rights of the child.

d) The Committee may make suggestions and general recommendations based on information received pursuant to articles 44 and 45 of this Convention. Such suggestions and general recommendations shall be transmitted to any State Party concerned and reported to the General Assembly, together with comments, if any, from States Parties.

PART III

Article 46

The present Convention shall be open for signature by all States.

Article 47

The present Convention is subject to ratification. Instruments of ratification shall be deposited with the Secretary-General of the United Nations.

Article 48

The present Convention shall remain open for accession by any State. The instruments of accession shall be deposited with the Secretary-General of the United Nations.

Article 49

1. The present Convention shall enter into force on the thirtieth day following the date of deposit with the Secretary-General of the United Nations of the twentieth instrument of ratification or accession.

2. For each State ratifying or acceding to the Convention after the deposit of the twentieth instrument of ratification or accession, the Convention shall enter into force on the thirtieth day after the deposit by such State of its instrument of ratification or accession.

Article 50

1. Any State Party may propose an amendment and file it with the Secretary-General of the United Nations. The Secretary-General shall thereupon communicate the proposed amendment to States Parties with a request that they indicate whether they favour a conference of States Parties for the purpose of considering and voting upon the proposals. In the event that within four months from the date of such communication at least one-third of the States Parties favour such a conference, the Secretary-General shall convene the conference under the auspices of the United Nations. Any amendment adopted by a majority of States Parties present and voting at the conference shall be submitted to the General Assembly of the United Nations for approval.

2. An amendment adopted in accordance with paragraph (1) of this article shall enter into force when it has been approved by the General Assembly of the United Nations and accepted by a two-thirds majority of States Parties.

3. When an amendment enters into force, it shall be binding on those States Parties which have accepted it, other States Parties still being bound by the provisions of this Convention and any earlier amendments which they have accepted.

Article 51

1. The Secretary-General of the United Nations shall receive and circulate to all States the text of reservations made by States at the time of ratification or accession.

2. A reservation incompatible with the object and purpose of the present Convention shall not be permitted.

3. Reservations may be withdrawn at any time by notification to this effect addressed to the Secretary-General of the United Nations who shall then inform all States. Such notification shall take effect on the date on which it is received by the Secretary-General.

Article 52

A State Party may denounce this Convention by written notification to the Secretary-General of the United Nations. Denunciation becomes effective one year after the date of receipt of the notification by the Secretary-General.

Article 53

The Secretary-General of the United Nations is designated as the depositary of the present Convention.

Article 54

The original of the present Convention, of which the Arabic, Chinese, English, French, Russian and Spanish texts are equally authentic, shall be deposited with the Secretary-General of the United Nations.

In witness thereof the undersigned plenipotentiaries, being duly authorised thereto by their respective governments, have signed the present Convention.

Appendix 2   UK Government Statement on Reservations

In March 1991, the Foreign and Commonwealth Office issued the following statement:

In reply to a Parliamentary Question from Mr Roger Simms MP, the Hon Mark Lennox-Boyd MP told the House of Commons on 21 March that the United Kingdom was making positive progress towards ratification of the Convention on the Rights of the Child. The Whitehall scrutiny of the text as regards the UK mainland has now taken place and Mr Lennox-Boyd outlined areas where it was envisaged that the UK would be making reservations on ratification.

Mr Lennox-Boyd said that the Whitehall review had been immensely valuable. It showed just how close our legislation concerning the protection of children was to this important international human rights standard.

'In particular, legislation on health and personal social services for children for which the Department of Health is responsible fully meets the relevant obligations of the Convention.

Regarding the articles within the Convention covering education, the United Kingdom again fully meets the requirements laid down and indeed in some cases exceeds them.

Naturally there are some differences between UK legislation and this wide ranging consensus document and we have identified the following areas where we envisage the need to make reservations when we come to ratify.

In some respects our legislation is more sophisticated than that contained in the Convention and one such area is that of Juvenile Custody. In England and Wales experience has shown that the mixing of adult and juvenile girls in custody can be mutually beneficial and 17 year old males are as a matter of course held with 18-20 year olds as young adult offenders. We will therefore be making a reservation to cover this aspect.

Similarly, because the provisions of the Convention regarding immigration and nationality are drafted in very broad terms, we will need to enter a reservation to reflect the way our own Immigration and Nationality laws operate.

It will also be necessary for the UK to enter a reservation in respect of the operation of the unique system of children's hearings in Scotland. Children's hearings in Scotland are informal and do not admit adversarial representation by lawyers. [This is under further consideration by the Scottish Office – June 1991].

In the field of employment too, the Convention definition of a child means that 16-18 years olds who are treated as young people under UK employment legislation would fall within its scope. We will need to make a reservation on this aspect: however our legislation more than matches the Convention's requirements on minimum age of employment and contains the necessary provision for enforcement and if need be prosecution for infringement of health and safety measures.

In one other area also – in relation to the termination of pregnancy – we envisage a reservation will be entered to avoid inconsistency with domestic legislation.

Our consultations will now continue with the Dependent Territories and the UK Islands to move as quickly as possible towards ratification of the Convention on the Rights of the Child.'

Appendix 3 Other United Nations International Instruments

United Nations Declaration of the Rights of the Child
adopted by the UN General Assembly 20 November 1959

...whereas mankind owes to the child the best it has to give.

Now therefore, the General Assembly proclaims this Declaration of the Rights of the Child to the end that he may have a happy childhood and enjoy for his own good and for the good of society the rights and freedoms herein set forth, and calls upon parents, upon men and women as individuals and upon voluntary organizations, local authorities and national governments to recognize these rights and strive for their observances by legislative and other measures progressively taken in accordance with the following principles:

Principle 1

The child shall enjoy all rights set forth in this Declaration. All children, without any exception whatsoever, shall be entitled to these rights, without distinction or discrimination on account of race, colour, sex, language, religion, political or other opinion, national or social origin, property, birth or other status, whether of himself or of his family.

Principle 2

The child shall enjoy special protection, and shall be given opportunities and facilities, by law and by other means, to enable him to develop physically, mentally, morally, spiritually and socially in a healthy and normal manner and in conditions of freedom and dignity. In the enactment of laws for this purpose the best interests of the child shall be the paramount consideration.

Principle 3

The child shall be entitled from his birth to a name and a nationality.

Principle 4

The child shall enjoy the benefits of social security. He shall be entitled to grow and develop in health; to this end special care and protection shall be provided both to him and to his mother, including adequate pre-natal and post-natal care. The child shall have the right to adequate nutrition, housing, recreation and medical services.

Principle 5

The child who is physically, mentally or socially handicapped shall be given the special treatment, education and care required by his particular condition.

Principle 6

The child, for the full and harmonious development of his personality, needs love and understanding. He shall, wherever possible, grow up in the care and under the responsibility of his parents, and in any case in an atmosphere of affection and of moral and material security; a child of tender years shall not, save in exceptional circumstances, be separated from his mother. Society and the public authorities shall have the duty to extend particular care to children without a family and to those without adequate means of support. Payment of state and other assistance toward the maintenance of children of large families is desirable.

Principle 7

The child is entitled to receive education, which shall be free and compulsory, at least in the elementary stages. He shall be given an education which will promote his general culture, and enable him on a basis of equal opportunity to develop his abilities, his individual judgement, and his sense of moral and social responsibility, and to become a useful member of society.

The best interests of the child shall be the guiding principle of those responsible for his education and guidance; that responsibility lies in the first place with his parents.

The child shall have full opportunity for play and recreation, which should be directed to the same purposes as education; society and the public authorities shall endeavour to promote the enjoyment of this right.

Principle 8

The child shall in all circumstances be among the first to receive protection and relief.

Principle 9

The child shall be protected against all forms of neglect, cruelty and exploitation. He shall not be subject of traffic, in any form.

The child shall not be admitted to employment before an appropriate minimum age; he shall in no case be caused or permitted to engage in any occupation or employment which would prejudice his health or education, or interfere with his physical, mental or moral development.

Principle 10

The child shall be protected from practices which may foster racial, religious and any other form of discrimination. He shall be brought up in a spirit of understanding, tolerance, friendship among people, peace and universal brotherhood and in full consciousness that his energy and talents should be devoted to the service of his fellow men.

The Universal Declaration of Human Rights
adopted by the UN General Assembly 10 December 1948

Relevant extracts

Article 25

1. Everyone has the right to a standard of living adequate for the health and well-being of himself and of his family, including food, clothing, housing and medical care and necessary social services, and the right to security in the event of unemployment, sickness, disability, widowhood, old age or other lack of livelihood in circumstances beyond his control.

2. Motherhood and childhood are entitled to special care and assistance. All children, whether born in or out of wedlock, shall enjoy the same social protection.

Article 26

1. Everyone has the right to education. Education shall be free, at least in the elementary and fundamental stages. Elementary education shall be compulsory. Technical and professional education shall be made generally available and higher education shall be equally accessible to all on the basis of merit.

2. Education shall be directed to the full development of the human personality and to the strengthening of respect for human rights and fundamental freedoms. It shall promote understanding, tolerance and friendship among all nations, racial or religious groups, and shall further the activities of the United Nations for the maintenance of peace.

3. Parents have a prior right to choose the kind of education that shall be given to their children.

International Covenant on Economic, Social and Cultural Rights
adopted by UN General Assembly 16 December 1966
Relevant extracts

Article 10

The States Parties to the present Covenant recognize that:

1. The widest possible protection and assistance should be accorded to the family, which is the natural and fundamental group unit of society, particularly for its establishment and while it is responsible for the care and education of dependent children. Marriage must be entered into with the free consent of the intending spouses.

2. Special protection should be accorded to mothers during a reasonable period before and after childbirth. During such period working mothers should be accorded paid leave or leave with adequate social security benefits.

3. Special measures of protection and assistance should be taken on behalf of all children and young persons without any discrimination for reasons of parentage or other conditions. Children and young persons should be protected from economic and social exploitation. Their employment in work harmful to their morals or health or dangerous to life or likely to hamper their normal development should be punishable by law. States should also set age limits below which the paid employment of child labour should be prohibited and punishable by law.

Article 11

1. The State Parties to the present Convenant recognize the right of everyone to an adequate standard of living for himself and his family, including adequate food, clothing and housing, and to the continuous improvement of living conditions. The States Parties will take appropriate steps to ensure the realization of this right, recognizing to this effect the essential importance of international co-operation based on free consent.

2. The States Parties to the present Covenant, recognizing the fundamental right of everyone to be free from hunger, shall take, individually and through international co-operation, the measures, including specific programmes, which are needed:

   (a) To improve methods of production, conservation and distribution of food by making full use of technical and scientific knowledge, by disseminating knowledge of the principles of nutrition and by developing or reforming agrarian systems in such a way as to achieve the most efficient development and utilization of natural resources;

   (b) Taking into account the problems of both food-importing and food-exporting countries, to ensure an equitable distribution of world food supplies in relation to need.

Article 12

1. The States Parties to the present Covenant recognize the right of everyone to the enjoyment of the highest attainable standard of physical and mental health.

2. The steps to be taken by the States Parties to the present Convenant to achieve the full realization of this right shall include those necessary for:

(a) The provision for the reduction of the still birth-rate and of infant mortality and for the healthy development of the child;

(b) The improvement of all aspects of environmental and industrial hygiene;

(c) The prevention, treatment and control of epidemic, endemic, occupational and other diseases;

(d) The creation of conditions which would assure to all medical service and medical attention in the event of sickness.

Article 13

1. The States Parties to the present Covenant recognize the right of everyone to education. They agree that education shall be directed to the full development of the human personality and the sense of its dignity, and shall strengthen the respect for human rights and fundamental freedoms. They further agree that education shall enable all persons to participate effectively in a free society, promote understanding, tolerance and friendship among all nations and all racial, ethnic or religious groups, and further the activities of the United Nations for the maintenance of peace.

2. The States Parties to the present Covenant recognize that, with a view to achieving the full realization of this right:

(a) Primary education shall be compulsory and available free to all;

(b) Secondary education in its different forms, including technical and vocational secondary education, shall be made generally available and accessible to all by every appropriate means, and in particular by the progressive introduction of free education;

(c) Higher education shall be made equally accessible to all, on the basis of capacity, by every appropriate means, and in particular by the progressive introduction of free education;

(d) Fundamental education shall be encouraged or intensified as far as possible for those persons who have not received or completed the whole period of their primary education;

(e) The development of a system of schools at all levels shall be actively pursued, an adequate fellowship system shall be established, and the material conditions of teaching staff shall be continuously improved.

3. The States Parties to the present Covenant undertake to have respect for the liberty of parents and, when applicable, legal guardians to choose for their children schools, other than those established by the public authorities, which conform to such minimum educational standards as may be laid down or approved by the State and to ensure the religious and moral education of their children in conformity with their own convictions.

4. No part of this article shall be construed so as to interfere with the liberty of individuals and bodies to establish and direct educational institutions, subject always to the observance of the principles set forth in paragraph 1 of this article and to the requirement that the education given in such institutions shall conform to such minimum standards as may be laid down by the State.

International Covenant on Civil and Political Rights
adopted by the UN General Assembly 16 December 1966

Relevant extracts

Article 23

1. The family is the natural and fundamental group unit of society and is entitled to protection by society and the State.

2. The right of men and women of marriageable age to marry and to found a family shall be recognized.

3. No marriage shall be entered into without the free and full consent of the intending spouses.

4. States Parties to the present Covenant shall take appropriate steps to equality of rights and responsibilities of spouses as to marriage, during marriage and at its dissolution. In the case of dissolution, provision shall be made for the necessary protection of any children.

Article 24

1. Every child shall have, without any discrimination as to race, colour, sex, language, religion, national or social origin, property or birth, the right to such measures of protection as are required by his status as a minor, on the part of his family, society and the State.

2. Every child shall be registered immediately after birth and shall have a name.

3. Every child has the right to acquire a nationality.

Appendix 4 Relevant European Instruments

The European Convention on Human Rights
Relevant extracts

Article 1

The High Contracting Parties shall secure to everyone within their jurisdiction the rights and freedoms defined in Section 1 of this Convention.

SECTION 1

Article 2

1. Everyone's right to life shall be protected by law. No one shall be deprived of his life intentionally save in the execution of a sentence of a court following his conviction of a crime for which this penalty is provided by law.

2. Deprivation of life shall not be regarded as inflicted in contravention of this Article when it results from the use of force which is no more than absolutely necessary:

   (a) in defence of any person from unlawful violence;

   (b) in order to effect a lawful arrest or to prevent the escape of a person lawfully detained;

   (c) in action lawfully taken for the purpose of quelling a riot or insurrection.

Article 3

No one shall be subjected to torture or to inhuman or degrading treatment or punishment.

Article 4

1. No one shall be held in slavery or servitude.

2. No one shall be required to perform forced or compulsory labour.

3. For the purpose of this Article the term 'forced or compulsory labour' shall not include:

   (a) any work required to be done in the ordinary course of detention imposed according to the provision of Article 5 of this Convention or during conditional release from such detention;

   (b) any service of a military character or, in case of conscientious objectors in countries where they are recognized, service exacted instead of compulsory military service;

(c) any service exacted in case of any emergency or calamity threatening the life or well-being of the community;

(d) any work or service which forms part of normal civic obligations.

Article 5

1. Everyone has the right to liberty and security of person. No one shall be deprived of his liberty save in the following cases and in accordance with a procedure prescribed by law:

(a) the lawful detention of a person after conviction by a competent court;

(b) the lawful arrest or detention of a person for non-compliance with the lawful order of a court or in order to secure the fulfilment of any obligation prescribed by law.

(c) the lawful arrest or detention of a person effected for the purpose of bringing him before the competent legal authority on reasonable suspicion of having committed an offence or when it is reasonably considered necessary to prevent his committing an offence of fleeing after having done so;

(d) the detention of a minor by lawful order for the purpose of educational supervison or his lawful detention for the purpose of bringing him before the competent legal authority;

(e) the lawful detention of persons for the prevention of the spreading of infectious diseases, of persons of unsound mind, alcoholics or drug addicts or vagrants;

(f) the lawful arrest or detention of a person to prevent his effecting an unauthorised entry into the country or of a person against who action is being taken with a view to deportation or extradition.

2. Everyone who is arrested shall be informed promptly, in a language which he understands, of the reasons for his arrest and of any charge against him.

3. Everyone arrested or detained in accordance with the provisions of paragraph 1(c) of this Article shall be brought promptly before a judge or other officer authorised by law to exercise judicial power and shall be entitled to trial within a reasonable time or to release pending trial. Release may be conditioned by guarantees to appear for trial.

4. Everyone who is deprived of his liberty by arrest or detention shall be entitled to take proceedings by which the lawfulness of his detention shall be decided speedily by a court and his release ordered if the detention is not lawful.

5. Everyone who has been the victim of arrest or detention in contravention of the provisions of this Article shall have an enforceable right to compensation.

Article 6

1. In the determination of his civil rights and obligations or of any criminal charge against him, everyone is entitled to a fair and public hearing within a reasonable time by an independent and impartial tribunal established by law. Judgement shall be pronounced publicly but the press and public may be excluded from all or part of the trial in the interest of morals, public order or national security in a democratic society, where the interests of juveniles or the protection of the private life of the parties so require, or to the extent strictly necessary in the opinion of the court in special circumstances where publcity would prejudice the interests of justice.

2. Everyone charged with a criminal offence shall be presumed innocent until proven guilty according to law.

3. Everyone charged with a criminal offence has the following minimum rights;

(a) to be informed promptly, in a language which he understands and in detail, of the nature and cause of the accusation against him;

(b) to have adequate time and facilities for the preparation of his defence;

(c) to defend himself in person or through legal assistance of his own choosing or, if he has not sufficient means to pay for legal assistance, to be given it free when the interests of justice so require;

(d) to examine or have examined witnesses against him and to obtain the attendance and examination of witnesses on his behalf under the same conditions as witnesses against him;

(e) to have the free assistance of an interpreter if he cannot understand or speak the langauge used in court.

Article 7

1. No one shall be held guilty of any criminal offence on account of any act or omission which did not constitute a criminal offence under national or international law at the time when it was committed. Nor shall a heavier penalty be imposed than the one that was applicable at the time the criminal offence was committed.

2. This Article shall not prejudice the trial and punishment of any person for any act or omission which at the time when it was committed, was criminal according to the general principles of law recognized by civilised nations.

Article 8

1. Everyone has the right to respect for his private and family life, his home and his correspondence.

2. There shall be no interference by a public authority with the exercise of this right except such as is in accordance with the law and is necessary in a democratic society in the interests of national security, public safety or the economic well-being of the country, for the prevention of disorder or crime, for the protection of health or morals, or for the protection of the rights and freedoms of others.

Article 9

1. Everyone has the right to freedom of thought, conscience and religion; this right includes freedom to change his religion or belief and freedom, either alone or in community with others and in public or private, to manifest his religion or belief, in worship, teaching, practice and observance.

2. Freedom to manifest one's religion or beliefs shall be subject only to such limitations as are prescribed by law and are necessary in a democratic society in the interests of public safety, for the protection of public order, health or morals, or for the protection of the rights and freedoms of others.

Article 10

1. Everyone has the right to freedom of expression. This right shall include freedom to hold opinions and to receive and impart information and ideas without interference by public authority and regardless of frontiers. The Article shall not prevent States from requiring the licensing of broadcasting, television or cinema enterprises.

2. The exercise of these freedoms, since it carries with it duties and responsibilities, may be subject to such formalities, conditions, restriction or penalties as are prescribed by law and are necessary in a democratic society, in the interests of national security, territorial integrity or public safety, for the prevention of disorder or crime, for the protection of health or morals, for the protection of the reputation or rights of others, for preventing the disclosure of information received in confidence, or for maintaining the authority and impartiality of the judiciary.

Article 11

1. Everyone has the right to freedom of peaceful assembly and to freedom of association with others, including the right to form and to join trade unions for the protection of his interests.

2. No restrictions shall be placed on the exercise of these rights other than such as are prescribed by law and are necessary in a democratic society in the interests of national security or public safety, for the prevention of disorder or crime, for the protection of health or morals or for the protection of the rights and freedoms of others. This Article shall not prevent the imposition of lawful restrictions on the exercise of these rights by members of the armed forces, of the police or of the administration of the State.

Article 12

Men and women of marriageable age have the right to marry and to found a family, according to the national laws governing the exercise of this right.

Article 13

Everyone whose rights and freedoms as set forth in this Convention are violated shall have an effective remedy before a national authority notwithstanding that the violation has been committed by persons acting in an official capacity.

Article 14

The enjoyment of the rights and freedoms set forth in this Convention shall be secured without discrimination on any ground such as sex, race, colour, language, religion, political or other opinion, national or social origin, association with a national minority, property, birth or other status.

Article 15

1. In time of war or other public emergency threatening the life of the nation any High Contracting Party may take measures derogating from its obligations under this Convention to the extent strictly required by the exigencies of the situation, provided that such measures are not inconsistent with its other obligations under international law.

2. No derogation from Article 2, except in respect of deaths resulting from lawful acts of war, or from Articles 3, 4 (paragraph 1) and 7 shall be made under this provision.

3. Any High Contracting Party availing itself of this right of derogation shall keep the Secretary General of the Council of Europe fully informed of the measures which it has taken and the reasons therefore. It shall also inform the Secretary General of the Council of Europe when such measures have ceased to operate and the provisions of the Convention are again being fully executed.

Article 16

Nothing in Articles 10, 11 and 14 shall be regarded as preventing the High Contracting Parties from imposing restrictions on the political activity of aliens.

Article 17

Nothing in this Convention may be interpreted as implying for any State, group or person any right to engage in any activity or perform any act aimed at the destruction of any of the rights and freedoms set forth herein or at their limitation to a greater extent than is provided for in the Convention.

Article 18

The restrictions permitted under this Convention to the said rights and freedoms shall not be applied for any purpose other than those for which they have been prescribed.

(Articles 19 to 66 cover the formation, procedure and powers of the European Commission and Court of Human Rights, the role of the Committee of Ministers of the Council of Europe, and the process of ratification and coming into force of the Convention.)

PROTOCOLS

FIRST PROTOCOL

Article 1

Every natural or legal person is entitled to the peaceful enjoyment of his possessions. No one shall be deprived of his possessions except in the public interest and subject to the conditions provided for by law and by the general principles of international law.

The preceding provisions shall not, however, in any way impair the right of a State to enforce such laws as it deems necessary to control the use of property in accordance with the general interest or to secure the payment of taxes or other contributions or penalties.

Article 2

No person shall be denied the right to education. In the exercise of any functions which it assumes in relation to education and to teaching, the State shall respect the right of parents to ensure such education and teaching in conformity with their own religious and philosophical convictions.

Article 3

The High Contracting Parties undertake to hold free elections at reasonable intervals by secret ballot, under conditions which will ensure the free expression of the opinion of the people in the choice of the legislature.

(Other articles cover procedure for ratification and coming into force of the Protocol.)

SECOND PROTOCOL

Gives the European Court the power to provide advisory opinions on the interpretation of the Convention, if asked to do so by the Committee of Ministers. This has not yet happened.

THIRD PROTOCOL

Modifies procedure for the implementation of the Convention.

FOURTH PROTOCOL

Mainly concerns right to freedom of movement – not ratified by UK due to immigration policy.

FIFTH PROTOCOL

Modifies procedure for the implementation of the Convention.

SIXTH PROTOCOL

Concerns abolition of the death penalty – in force since 1985 and ratified by Austria, Denmark, France, Iceland, Luxembourg, Netherlands, Portugal, Spain and Sweden, but not the UK.

SEVENTH PROTOCOL

Not yet in force; concerns appeal rights against expulsion of aliens and against conviction for criminal offences; rights to compensation for wrongful conviction; right not to be tried more than once, etc.

EIGHTH PROTOCOL

Not yet in force; modifies procedure for the implementation of the Convention.

The European Social Charter

The European Social Charter is intended to provide economic and social rights as a counterpart to the European Human Rights Convention. A majority of the member states of the Council of Europe have ratified the charter, including the UK. But in doing so the UK has indicated non-acceptance of parts of five significant articles, including several parts of the article aiming to provide protection for young people.

Article 7 of the Charter covers 'The Right of Children and Young People to Protection', but of the 10 paragraphs, the UK has not accepted three (see paragraphs printed in italics below).

Article 7

The right of children and young persons to protection
With a view to ensuring the effective exercise of the right of children and young persons to protection, the Contracting Parties undertake:

1. *to provide that the minimum age of admission to employment shall be 15 years, subject to exceptions for children employed in prescribed light work without harm to their health, morals or education;*

2. to provide that a higher minimum age of admission to employment shall be fixed with respect to prescribed occupations regarded as dangerous or unhealthy;

3. to provide that persons who are still subject to compulsory education shall not be employed in such work as would deprive them of the full benefit of their education;

4. *to provide that the working hours of persons under 16 years of age shall be limited in accordance with the needs of their development, and particularly with their need for vocational training;*

5. to recognise the right of young workers and apprentices to a fair wage or other appropriate allowances;

6. to provide that the time spent by young persons in vocational training during the normal working hours with the consent of the employer shall be treated as forming part of the working day;

7. *to provide that employed persons of under 18 years of age shall be entitled to not less than three weeks' annual holiday with pay;*

8. to provide that persons under 18 years of age shall not be employed in night work with the exception of certain occupations provided for by national laws or regulations;

9. to provide that persons under 18 years of age employed in occupations prescribed by national laws or regulations shall be subject to regular medical control;

10. to ensure special protection against physical and moral dangers to which children and young persons are exposed, and particularly against those resulting directly or indirectly from their work.

Other Conventions

There are three other European conventions of relevance to children and young people:

The European Convention on the Adoption of Children (ratified by the UK in 1967);

The European Convention on the Legal Status of Children Born out of Wedlock (ratified by the UK with reservations in 1981);

The European Convention on the Enforcement of Decisions Concerning the Custody of Children (ratified by the UK in 1986).

(A wide variety of publications about the European Conventions are available from the Council of Europe Publications section, Council of Europe, Boite Postale 431, R6, Strasbourg 67006 Cedex, France. The Children's Legal Centre publishes an information sheet on the European Convention on Human Rights, CLC, 20 Compton Terrace, London, N1 2UN.)

Appendix 5 Useful materials available on the Convention on the Rights of the Child

CANTWELL, N. (1989)
Advocacy and education: a tool for the implementation of the UN Convention? Paper presented at the International Conference on Making Reality of Children's Rights – Stockholm, 11–12 June 1989. Geneva: Defence for Children International. 7pp.

CANTWELL, N. (1989)
Content with the content? A review of what the future Convention says and means. Conference on the Convention on the Rights of the Child, International Catholic Child Bureau – Chantilly, France, 28-30th September 1989. Geneva: Defence for Children International. 4pp.

CANTWELL, N. (1989)
The Convention on the Rights of the Child: a review of the content. Geneva: Defence for Children International. 7pp.

CANTWELL, N. (1988)
The future Convention on the Rights of the Child: a lesson in investment. Geneva: Defence for Children International. 10pp.

CANTWELL, N. (1990)
How NGOs contributed to drafting the Convention on the Rights of the Child. Symposium on the Contribution of NGOs to the Formulation and Promotion of International Human Rights Law – 4 May 1990, Geneva. Geneva: Defence for Children International. 7pp.

CANTWELL, N. (1989)
The importance of the Convention for work on behalf of children: summary of presentation. Press Seminar on the future Convention on the Rights of the Child, UNICEF – Geneva, 16 November 1989. Geneva: Defence for Children International. 3pp.

CANTWELL, N. (1988)
The importance of the Convention on the Rights of the Child: an NGO perspective. Paper presented at the Seminar on the Convention on the Rights of the Child – Oslo, Norway, 23 March 1988. Geneva: Defence for Children International. 3pp.

CASTELLE, K. (1989)
In the child's best interest: a primer on the U.N. Convention on the Rights of the Child. New rev. ed. East Greenwich (USA): Foster Parents Plan International & Defence for Children International. 46pp.

DEFENCE FOR CHILDREN INTERNATIONAL, and UNICEF (1989)
The future United Nations Convention on the Rights of the Child. 3rd ed. Geneva: DCI and UNICEF. 1 pack. (Contains various leaflets outlining the Convention and a draft copy of the Convention).

NGO GROUP FOR THE CONVENTION ON THE RIGHTS OF THE CHILD (1990)
Children's rights and you: a short introduction to the Convention on the Rights of the Child. Geneva: The Group. 8pp.

SAVE THE CHILDREN FUND (1990)
The UN Convention on the Rights of the Child. A seminar convened by Save the Children Fund – Scotland. Glasgow: The Fund. 1 pack. (Conference pack which includes copy of the Convention).

UNICEF, and UNITED NATIONS CENTRE FOR HUMAN RIGHTS (1990)
Children's rights need international protection. Geneva: UNICEF and the Centre. 1 leaflet. (Brief summary of Convention and its objectives).

UNICEF-UK, and SAVE THE CHILDREN (1990)
Teachers handbook: teaching the UN Convention on the Rights of the Child. London: UNICEF-UK and SCF. 30pp.

UNICEF-UK, and SAVE THE CHILDREN (1990)
The whole child: a project to introduce the UN Convention on the Rights of the Child to 8-13 year-olds. London: UNICEF-UK and SCF. 54pp. (Participation articles).

UNITED NATIONS CENTRE FOR HUMAN RIGHTS, and UNICEF (1990)
Convention on the Rights of the Child: information kit. Geneva: The Centre and UNICEF. 1 pack. (A pack containing leaflets on various aspects of the Convention, plus a copy of the Convention itself).

UNITED NATIONS CENTRE FOR HUMAN RIGHTS, and UNICEF (1989)
The future United Nations Convention on the Rights of the Child: media kit. Geneva: The Centre and UNICEF. 1 pack. (Contains leaflets on various aspects of the future Convention and a draft copy of the Convention).

UNITED NATIONS. Centre for Human Rights (1990)
The rights of the child. Geneva: The Centre. 32pp. (Human rights – fact sheet, no. 10). (Includes a copy of the Convention on the Rights of the Child).

UNITED NATIONS (1989)
The Convention on the Rights of the Child. Adopted by the General Assembly of the United Nations on 20 November 1989. Geneva: Defence for Children International and the United Nations Children's Fund. 16pp.

VITTACHI, A. (1989)
Stolen childhood: in search of the rights of the child. Cambridge: Polity Press in association with North-South Productions and Channel Four. 159pp.

VITTACHI, A. (1990)
Stolen childhood: the rights of the child. Based on a series produced in conjunction with Channel Four. London: North South Productions. 24pp.

References

(1) Gillick v West Norfolk and Wisbech AHA [1986] AC112.

(2) Scottish Law Commission, *Report on the Legal Capacity and Responsibility of Minors and Pupils.* HMSO:1987.

(3) Children's Legal Centre, *At What Age Can I...?* (Children's Legal Centre Information Sheet). 1991.

(4) Lowe, N.V. and White, R.A.H., *Wards of Court.* 2nd ed. Barry Rose:1986.

(5) Scottish Office, *Review of Scottish Child Care Law.* HMSO:1990.

(6) Department of Education and Science, *The Education (Special Educational Needs) (Approval of Independent Schools) Regulations.* 1991.

(7) Grant, J.P., *The State of the World's Children. 1991.* Oxford University Press for UNICEF:1991.

(8) OECD, *Development Co-operation – Efforts and Policies of the Members of the Development Assistance Committee, OECD.* 1990.

(9) see (1).

(10) Scottish Law Commission, *Parental Responsibilities and Rights, Guardianship and the Administration of Children's Property.* 1990.

(11) Department of Health, *The Welfare of Children in Hospital.* (Draft Circular).1990.

(12) British Paediatric Association and British Association of Perinatal Paediatrics, *Categories of Babies Receiving Neonatal Care.* BPA:1984.

(13) Fenton, A.C. and Field, D.J., Shortfall of Equipment for Neonatal Intensive Care and the Introduction of Budget Holding Contracts. *British Medical Journal,* 301(6745):1990. p201-203.

(14) North West Regional Health Authority Medical Committee, Paediatric Sub-Committee, *Statement on Reduction in Intensive Care Cots at the Perinatal Centre, St Mary's Hospital, Manchester.* 1988.

(15) Royal College of Physicians, *Medical Care of the Newborn in England and Wales.* 1988.

(16) United Kingdom Children's Cancer Study Group, *Report on Cancer Services for Children.* 1987.

(17) Children's Legal Centre, *A Right to Life Protected by Law.* (Children's Legal Centre Briefing). 1988.

(18) European Commission of Human Rights, Application No.7154/75, Association X v UK. Strasbourg: Decision of the Commission: 12 July 1978.

(19) Office of Population Censuses and Surveys, *Mortality Statistics:Perinatal and Infant: Social and Biological Factors, 1987.* HMSO:1990.

(20) Department of Health, *Infant and Perinatal Mortality at an All-Time Low* (Press Release: 9 October 1990).

(21) National Children's Bureau, Policy and Practice Review Group, *Investing in the Future : Child Health Ten Years After the Court Report.* National Children's Bureau:1987.

(22) Joint Council for the Welfare of Immigrants, *Children Born in the UK – Nationality and Immigration.* 1986.

(23) Department of Health, *Inter-Departmental Review of Adoption Law.* 1990.

(24) Royal College of Obstetricians and Gynaecologists, *Donor Insemination.* 1987.

(25) European Court of Human Rights, Gaskin v UK. Strasbourg: judgment : 7 July 1989.

(26) European Court of Human Rights, Johnston and others. Strasbourg: judgment : 18 December 1986.

(27) European Commission of Human Rights, Gaskin v UK. Strasbourg: Report of the Commission adopted : 13 November 1987.

(28) Department of Social Security, *Children Come First : The Government's Proposals on the Maintenance of Children.* HMSO:1990.

(29) Commission for Racial Equality, *Immigration Control Procedures: Report of a Formal Investigation.* 1985.

(30) European Court of Human Rights, Berrehab v Netherlands. Strasbourg: judgement : 21 June 1988.

(31) European Commission of Human Rights, Fadele v UK. Strasbourg: Admissibility decision on application number 13078/87: 12 February 1990.

(32) Divided Families Campaign, *Give Us A Happy Ending : How Families Are Kept Apart By British Immigration Law.* 1990.

(33) United Kingdom Immigrants Advisory Service, *Annual Report, 1987/88.*

(34) Re-Unite (National Council for Abducted Children) , *The Charter for Abducted Children.* 1990.

(35) see (10).

(36) see (1).

(37) European Commission of Human Rights, Barbara Stevens v UK. Strasbourg: Decision on Admissibility of Application 11674/85: March 1986.

(38) American Civil Liberties Union, *The Rights of Students : An American Civil Liberties Union Handbook.* Avon Books:1977.

(39) Mandla v Dowell Lee (1983) 1 All ER 1062, HL.

(40) see (2).

(41) see (1).

(42) Department of Education and Science, *Education for All : The Report of the Committee of Inquiry into the Education of Children from Ethnic Minority Groups.* (Swann Report). HMSO:1985.

(43) see (1).

(44) *The Guardian,* Disabled Boy Forces Sun to Pay for 'Worst Brat' libel. 24 May 1991.

(45) European Court of Human Rights, Leander case.
     Strasbourg: judgment : 27 March 1987.

(46) see (10).

(47) European Commission, *Proposal for a Council Directive on Parental Leave and Leave for Family Reasons.*
     (COM(83)686).1983.

(48) Smyth, M. and Robus, N., *The Financial Circumstances of Families With Disabled Children Living in Private Households.*
     (OPCS Surveys of Disability, no.5). HMSO:1989.

(49) Jaspert, J., Cavanagh. S. and Debono, J., *Thinking of Small Children : Access, Provision and Play.* We Welcome Small Children Campaign/Women's Design Service : 1988.

(50) Moss, P., *Childcare in the European Community 1985-1990.*
     Commission of the European Communities : 1990.

(51) National Children's Bureau, Under Fives Unit, *Statistics : Under Fives and Pre-School Services, 1989.* Under Fives Unit : 1991.

(52) National Children's Bureau, Under Fives Unit, *A Policy for Young children : A Framework for Action.* 1990.

(53) Butler-Sloss, E., *Report of the Inquiry into Child Abuse in Cleveland 1987.* HMSO: 1988.

(54) Department of Health, *Children and Young Persons on Child Protection Registers, Year Ending 31 March 1989, England.*
     (AF 89/13) DH:1990.

(55) *ChildLine : the Second Year.* ChildLine : 1989.

(56) Hillman, M., Adams, J., and Whitelegg J., *One False Move :- A Study of Children's Independent Mobility.* Policy Studies Institute : 1990.

(57) Department of Health, Social Services Inspectorate, *Child Protection in London : Aspects of Management Arrangements in Social Services Departments.* The Inspectorate : 1990.

(58) Wandsworth Area Child Protection Committee, *The Report of the Stephanie Fox Practice Review.* LB Wandsworth : 1990.

(59) Newson J. and E., *The Extent of Parental Physical Punishment in the UK.* APPROACH : 1989.

(60) Committee of Ministers of the Council of Europe, *Violence in the Family : Recommendation No. R(85)4,* adopted by the Committee of Ministers on 26 March 1985. Strasbourg : Council of Europe : 1986.

(61) End Physical Punishment of Children (EPOCH) , *List of Supporting Organisations.* Unpublished : 1991.

(62) see (10).

(63) see (23).

(64) see (2).

(65) Re P (adoption application No.344 of 1987), *Adoption & Fostering,* Vol.13, No.1, pp.54-55: 1989.

(66) Finlay, R., *Unaccompanied Refugee Children :- a Monitoring Report.* The Refugee Council : 1990.

(67) Refugee Council, Working Group on Unaccompanied Refugee Children and Adolescents, *Better Child Care for Unaccompanied Refugee Children and Adolescents to the UK.* Unpublished : 1990.

(68) United Nations High Commissioner for Refugees, *Handbook on Procedures and Criteria for Determining Refugee Status.* Geneva: UNHCR : 1988.

(69) Office of Population Censuses and Surveys, *Disabled Children : Services, Transport and Education* (OPCS Surveys of Disability in Great Britain No.6). HMSO : 1989.

(70) Inner London Education Authority, Research and Statistics Branch, *Characteristics of Pupils in Special Schools and Units : a Survey.* (RS 962/84). ILEA : 1984. (rev. ed. RS 1198/88 available from London Residuary Body).

(71) Swann, W., *Variations Between LEAs in Levels of Segregation in Special Schools, 1982 – 1990 : Preliminary Report.* Centre for Studies on Integration in Education : 1991.

(72) Department of Health, *An Epidemiological Overview of Child Health.* Unpublished : 1990.

(73) Department of Health, *The Diets of British School Children.* HMSO : 1989.

(74) Bradshaw, J., *Child Poverty and Deprivation in the UK.* National Children's Bureau : 1990.

(75) Kleinman, J.C., and Kieley, J.L., *Postneonatal Mortality in the United States : an International Perspective.* National Center for Health Statistics, Hyattsville, USA. Unpublished : 1990.

(76) Woodroffe, C., and Kurtz, Z., *Working for Children ? Children's Services and the NHS Review.* National Children's Bureau : 1989.

(77) Macfarlane, J.A., and Pillay, U., Who does What, and How Much in the Pre-School Child Health Services in England, *British Medical Journal*, Vol.289, No.6448, pp.851-2 : 1984.

(78) Department of Health, Unpublished memorandum to author : 1991.

(79) quoted in Bradshaw, J., *Child Poverty and Deprivation in the UK.* see (74).

(80) *Official Journal of the European Communities*, Action brought on 30 October 1989 by the Commission against the UK : Case C-337/89.

(81) *Official Journal of the European Communities*, Action brought on 7 March 1990 by the Commission against the UK : Case C-56/90.

(82) Children's Legal Centre, Children and the Environment, *Childright*, No.59, pp.9-16 : 1989.

(83) Dyer, C., Australian Court Rules Passive Smoking Harmful, *British Medical Journal*, Vol.302, No.6773, p.369 : 1991.

(84) Platt, S.D., and others, Damp Housing, Mould Growth, and Symptomatic Health State. *British Medical Journal*, Vol.298, No.6689, pp.1673-8 : 1989.

(85) Beral, V., Leukaemia and Nuclear Installations : Occupational Exposure of Fathers to Radiation may be the Explanation, *British Medical Journal*, Vol.300, No.6722, pp.411-2 : 1990.

(86) see (7).

(87) OPCS, *Deaths from Accidents and Violence*. (DH4 Series). OPCS:1988.

(88) Child Accident Prevention Trust, *Child Pedestrian Accidents*. (CAPT Factsheet). The Trust : 1991.

(89) Livingstone, A., Female circumcision, a Continuing Problem in Britain, *British Medical Journal*, Vol.302, No.6774, pp.477-8 : 1991.

(90) Schmitt, B.D., *Your Child's Health : a Paediatric Guide for Parents*. New York : Bantam Books : 1987.

(91) Leach, P., *Babyhood*. 2nd. ed. Penguin : 1983.

(92) British Overseas Aid, *Annual Review*.

(93) see (5).

(94) Stewart, G., and Tutt, N., *Children in Custody*. Avebury:1987.

(95) see (74).

(96) Oppenheim, C., *Poverty the Facts*. Child Poverty Action Group : 1990.

(97) National Association of Citizens Advice Bureaux, *Income Support and 16 – 17 Year Olds*. (Evidence Series E/5/89). NACAB:1989.

(98) see (74).

(99) Bradshaw, J., and Holmes H., *Living on the Edge : a Study of the Living Standards of Families on Benefit in Tyne and Wear*. Tyneside Child Poverty Action Group : 1989.

(100) Evason, E., *On the Edge : a Study of Poverty and Long Term Unemployment in Northern Ireland*. CPAG : 1986.

(101) Bradshaw, J., and Morgan, J., *Budgeting on Benefit*. Family Policy Studies Centre : 1987.

(102) see (99).

(103) Central Statistical Office, *Social Trends 20*. HMSO : 1990.

(104) Association of Metropolitan Authorities, *A Strategy for Racial Equality in Housing – A Policy and Good Practice Guide for Local Authorities. No.2, Homelessness*. 1990.

(105) National Association of Citizens Advice Bureaux, *Homelessness – A National Survey of Citizens Advice Bureaux Clients.* (Evidence Series, E/2/88). 1988.

(106) HM Inspectorate, *Standards in Education 1988-1989 : The Annual Report of HM Senior Chief Inspector of Schools.* Department of Education and Science : 1990.

(107) Department of Education and Science, *Education Statistics for the United Kingdom, 1989.* HMSO : 1990.

(108) European Commission of Human Rights, Application No.14229/88, X and Y v UK. Admissibility Decision : 13 December 1990; Application No.13134/87, Wendy and Jeremy Costello v UK. Admissibility Decision : 13 December 1990.

(109) Commission for Racial Equality, *Birmingham Local Authority and Schools : Referral and Suspension of Pupils : Report of a Formal Investigation.* 1985.

(110) National Curriculum Council, *Education for Citizenship* (Curriculum Guidance Series, No.8). 1990.

(111) Council of Europe, Committee of Ministers, *Teaching and Learning About Human Rights in Schools.* 1985.

(112) Commission for Racial Equality, *Code of Practice for the Elimination of Racial Discrimination in Schools.* 1989.

(113) European Commission, *The Education of Children of Migrant Workers.* (Directive 77/486/EEC). 1977.

(114) European Commission, *Report on the Implementation in Member States of Directive 77/486/EEC.* 1989.

(115) Commission for Racial Equality, *Ethnic Minority School Teachers: a Survey in Eight Local Education Authorities.* 1989.

(116) European Parliament, *Resolution on Freedom of Education in the European Community.* 1984.

(117) Debell, Sevket and Teh v London Borough of Bromley (Bromley County Court) 12 November 1984.

(118) Times Educational Supplement, *Keeping the Issues Out of Geography* (editorial article). 3890, 18 Jan. 1991, p.19 : 1991.

(119) see (56).

(120) National Association for the Care and Resettlement of Offenders, *A Review of the Play and Recreational Needs of Young People Growing Up on Housing Estates.* 1988.

(121) Kids' Clubs Network, *A Patchwork of Provision.* 1990.

(122) International Association for the Child's Right to Play, *Declaration of the Child's Right to Play.* Rev. ed.1989.

(123) Pond, C., and Searle, A., *The Hidden Army : Children at Work in the 1990s.* Low Pay Unit : 1991.

(124) Scottish Low Pay Unit, *Working Children Project.* (SLPU Briefing Paper No.3). 1990.

(125) Home Office, Standing Conference on Crime Prevention, *Report of the Working Group on Young People and Alcohol.* Home Office : 1987.

(126) Goddard, E., *Smoking Among Secondary School Children in 1988 : Enquiry Carried Out by OPCS on behalf of the Department of Health.* HMSO : 1989.

(127) OPCS, Drinking in England and Wales. OPCS : 1987. (reported in *The NCH Factfile – Children in Danger 1990.* London : National Children's Home : 1990).

(128) Gillie, O., Child Slaves put to Work in Britain, *The Independent,* 6 April, 1990.

(129) Department of Health, *Local Research Ethics Committees.* Draft Health Circular, October 1989.

(130) European Commission of Human Rights, Mrs X v UK. Strasbourg : Report adopted by the Commission, 17 December 1981.

(131) European Commission of Human Rights, Mrs X and Miss X v UK. Strasbourg: Report adopted by the Commission, 18 July 1986.

(132) Levy, A., and Kahan, B., *The Pindown Experience and the Protection of Children. The Report of the Staffordshire Child Care Inquiry* : Staffordshire County Council: 1991.

(133) Department of Health Social Services Inspectorate, *Inspection of Youth Treatment Services 1988 Overview Report.* DH : 1988.

(134) NHS Health Advisory Service, *Bridges Over Troubled Waters : a Report from the NHS Health Advisory Service on Services for Disturbed Adolescents*. HAS : 1986.

(135) National Association for the Care and Resettlement of Offenders, *Detention in a Young Offender Institution : the First Year*. NACRO : 1989.

(136) Amnesty International, *Alleged forced Admissions During Incommunicado Detention*. Amnesty International : 1988.

(137) see (1).

(138) International Conventions for the Protection of Victims of War – the four Geneva Conventions, established August 12 1949. Protocols Additional to the Geneva Conventions, established 10 June 1977. Geneva : International Committee of the Red Cross.

(139) *Hansard*, 27 November 1990, Col.338.

(140) Ministry of Defence, Unpublished memorandum to author. March 1991.

(141) House of Commons, *Special Report from the Select Committee on the Armed Forces Bill*. (Paper 179). HMSO : 1991.

(142) see (53).

(143) Home Office, Cautions, Court Proceedings and Sentencing in 1988, *Home Office Statistical Bulletin*, No.21 : 1989.

(144) Landau, S.F., and Nathan, F., Selecting Delinquents for Cautioning in the London Metropolitan Area, *British Journal of Criminology*, Vol.23, No.2, pp.128-49 : 1983.

(145) Greater London Council, *Policing London*, No.13 : 1982.

(146) NACRO Juvenile Crime Committee, *Diverting Juvenile Offenders from Prosecution*. NACRO : 1989.

(147) see (1).

Index of
Bills and Acts of Parliament

This index is in word-by-word alphabetical order and covers Bills and Acts of Parliament cited in the text. There is a separate index to names and subjects. Numbers in **bold** type indicate the main source of information.

Index of
subjects and names

This index is in word-by-word alphabetical order and covers subjects, persons and bodies mentioned in the main text and Appendixes 2,3 and 4. It does **not** cover the restatement of each Article of the Convention and summary thereof in Appendix 1. There is a separate index to Bills and Acts of Parliament. Figures in **bold** type indicate the main source of information.